Nick Bano is a barrister at Garden Court Chambers, who has been involved in bringing many of the significant PSED challenges in the field of housing law. He appeared in the key case of *Forward v Aldwyck*, as well as more recent and housing-specific matters such as *TM v Metropolitan*, *London & Quadrant v Patrick* and *Adesotu v Lewisham*.

A Practical Guide to the Public Sector Equality Duty in Housing

A Practical Guide to the Public Sector Equality Duty in Housing

Nick Bano

Law Brief Publishing

Published 2023 by Law Brief Publishing, an imprint of Law Brief Publishing Ltd
30 The Parks
Minehead
Somerset
TA24 8BT

www.lawbriefpublishing.com

Paperback: 978-1-914608-60-5

This book is dedicated to the tenants with disabilities whom I have represented in the course of (inadvertently) preparing it. I am honoured that they put their trust in me, particularly at such fraught moments in their lives. It is dedicated in particular to the parents and siblings of TM, who have fought for him with such determination, bravery and compassion.

PREFACE

Granting permission to appeal in *Forward v Aldwyck* in 2019, McCombe LJ said: 'These PSED questions in housing matters continue to throw up points of principle on which guidance is required'. He was right then, but even the Court of Appeal's subsequent decision in *Forward* did not put the matter to bed. Since then there has been a steady flow of PSED authorities in the social housing possession context alone. The PSED has also become the *leitmotif* of homelessness challenges, and is frequently raised in allocations cases, accommodation judicial reviews and housing management matters.

In different contexts, the PSED has been held to add nothing substantive, or to fundamentally change the complexion of a case. It has been treated as a makeweight by some, and a key part of anti-discrimination protection by others. It can add pointless complexity to proceedings, or persuade a public authority to change its decision at an early stage. Outcomes have been dramatically reversed on appeal, when different judges have come to look at the very same facts. The law reports are beginning to groan with authorities that could assist either side of a dispute. As one High Court judge described the state of the case law when deciding an appeal from a possession case: 'any court considering the scope of the PSED is provided with an embarrassment of riches'[1].

Where, when and how best to deploy PSED arguments will always be a matter of professional judgment. But the aim of this book is to try to make some sense of the often-Janus-faced authorities: to identify the more fundamental, immutable aspects of the duty, and to firm up some of its more nebulous characteristics.

In all of the PSED cases in which I have played some part, it has been a great pleasure to work with some of the sharpest and most knowledgeable

1 *Patrick v London & Quadrant HT* [2020] HLR 3, [2019] EWHC 1263 (QB), per Turner J at [21].

lawyers in the fields of housing and equality rights. I benefitted greatly from working with leaders including Karon Monaghan KC, Liz Davies KC, Stephanie Harrison KC and Toby Vanhegan. Matthew Lee and David Renton are also infinite sources of learning and encouragement on PSED and equality matters. I owe a great deal to my regular opponents, many of whom respond to disability issues with great sensitivity and judiciousness. I have gained so much from all of my colleagues, but any errors or misunderstandings, though, are obviously down to me.

The contents of this book are believed to be correct and up-to-date at 3rd January 2023. It is assumed that the reader is familiar with the underlying issues of housing, homelessness and public law. This book is not designed to be read in isolation, and only addresses the specific PSED issues that overlap with or complement those substantive matters.

Nick Bano
January 2023

CONTENTS

CHAPTER ONE

PRELIMINARY POINTS

1.1 The current duty in context

The Public Sector Equality Duty is contained in section 149 of the Equality Act 2010. The 2010 Act collated and expanded the scope of three similar duties that had been specific to race, disability and sex legislation: section 71 of the Race Relations Act 1976; section 49A of the Disability Discrimination Act 1975; and section 76A of the Sex Discrimination Act 1975.

When the Equality Bill 2009 was introduced, those three duties had only been inserted relatively recently[1]. The Race Relations Act duty had been created earliest, in 2000, as a method of implementing the recommendations of the 1999 Macpherson Inquiry into the murder of Stephen Lawrence, which contained the first official acknowledgment of institutional racism in the Metropolitan Police[2]. The intention was to move away from a system of reactive 'fault-based' liability, and towards a proactive obligation on public authorities to identify and remedy structural disadvantages[3]. It seems that there was then a desire throughout the early 2000s to roll out that Race Relations Act model

---

1 By section 2 of the Race Relations (Amendment) Act 2000, section 13 of the Disability Discrimination Act 2005, and section 84 the Equality Act 2006 respectively.

2 *R (Bridges) v Chief Constable of South Wales Police* [2020] 1 WLR 5064, [2020] EWCA Civ 1058, per Sir Terence Etherton MR, Dame Victoria Sharp PQBD & Singh LJ at [177-179].

3 Ibid. at [178], citing Karon Monaghan KC, *Equality Law* (second edition, 2013) at para. 16.06.

more widely, first to disability and sex, and then across the board. The 2009 Equality Bill, which contained the first generalised PSED, was large and complex, and was one of the last acts of the Blair/Brown governments: it gained Royal Assent less than a month before the 2010 general election.

It contained a new Public Sector Equality Duty under section 149: a single duty, which applies to all public functions right across the eight protected characteristics listed in sub-section 149(7). It came into force on 5th April 2011[4]. However, from the outset, the courts continued to apply the older jurisprudence relating to the predecessor duties[5], and the pre-2011 cases are still frequently cited.

1.2 The duty

Section 149 of the Equality Act 2010 provides that:

> "**Public sector equality duty**
>
> (1) A public authority must, in the exercise of its functions, have due regard to the need to—
>
> > (a) eliminate discrimination, harassment, victimisation and any other conduct that is prohibited by or under this Act;
> >
> > (b) advance equality of opportunity between persons who share a relevant protected characteristic and persons who do not share it;

---

4 SI 2011/1066 art. 2(a).

5 See e.g. *R (Hurley & Moore) v Secretary of State for Business, Education & Skills* [2012] HRLR 13, [2012] EWHC 201 (Admin) per Elias LJ at [71-72]; *Barnsley MBC v Norton* [2012] PTSR 54, [2011] EWCA Civ 834 (the litigation in *Norton* overlapped with the PSED's commencement date, and both the old section 49A duty and the new PSED are cited).

(c) foster good relations between persons who share a relevant protected characteristic and persons who do not share it.

(2) A person who is not a public authority but who exercises public functions must, in the exercise of those functions, have due regard to the matters mentioned in subsection (1).

(3) Having due regard to the need to advance equality of opportunity between persons who share a relevant protected characteristic and persons who do not share it involves having due regard, in particular, to the need to—

(a) remove or minimise disadvantages suffered by persons who share a relevant protected characteristic that are connected to that characteristic;

(b) take steps to meet the needs of persons who share a relevant protected characteristic that are different from the needs of persons who do not share it;

(c) encourage persons who share a relevant protected characteristic to participate in public life or in any other activity in which participation by such persons is disproportionately low.

(4) The steps involved in meeting the needs of disabled persons that are different from the needs of persons who are not disabled include, in particular, steps to take account of disabled persons' disabilities.

(5) Having due regard to the need to foster good relations between persons who share a relevant protected characteristic and persons who do not share it involves having due regard, in particular, to the need to—

(a) tackle prejudice, and

(b) promote understanding.

(6) Compliance with the duties in this section may involve treating some persons more favourably than others; but that is not to be taken as permitting conduct that would otherwise be prohibited by or under this Act.

(7) The relevant protected characteristics are—

- age;
- disability;
- gender reassignment;
- pregnancy and maternity;
- race;
- religion or belief;
- sex;
- sexual orientation.

(8) A reference to conduct that is prohibited by or under this Act includes a reference to—

(a) a breach of an equality clause or rule;

(b) a breach of a non-discrimination rule.

(9) Schedule 18 (exceptions) has effect".

Sub-sections (1)(a)-(c) contain the three 'equality aims'. These are the ultimate objectives that the PSED seeks to encourage local authorities to work towards achieving. The way that the PSED works is that it obliges public authorities to have 'due regard' to the need to meet those three equality aims. This is quite a convoluted, soft turn of phrase, but happily for practitioners the courts have used more concrete and precise language to describe compliance with this duty, as we shall see throughout this book. To cite, for the moment, just one of the many judicial statements describing the purpose of the duty: the Court of Appeal has said that the PSED 'is designed to secure the brighter illumination of a person's disability so that, to the extent that it bears upon his rights under other laws, it attracts a full appraisal'[6].

Sub-section (2) contains an expanded definition of the concept of 'the functions of a public authority', which includes any public functions carried out by a body which is not itself a public authority. Possession proceedings and allocations decisions brought or made by registered social landlords are, depending on the circumstances such as the size of the landlord's stock, likely to constitute public functions[7].

Sub-sections (3) to (6) set out the specific ways in which public authorities are required to carry out the general 'due regard' duty contained in sub-section (1). Sub-section (7) then contains the relevant protected characteristics (see 1.3 below).

Importantly, section 149 does not amend any other legislative provisions. It does not grant any new powers to public authorities, or even modify any existing ones, but it complements or enhances the way in which public authorities carry out their functions. For example, the PSED does not suddenly require local authorities to accommodate a person with a disability who would not otherwise be entitled to housing. Instead, where there is a pre-existing matter of discretion or evaluative judgment for a local authority, or where it is preparing a policy or taking a nuanced decision, the PSED will feed into the way in which the decision is reached, or possibly merely alert the authority to the existence of

---

6 *Pieretti v Enfield LBC* [2011] PTSR 565, [2010] EWCA Civ 1104, per Wilson LJ at [26].

7 See e.g. *R (TRX) v Network Homes Ltd* [2022] EWHC 456 (Admin), applying *R (Weaver) v London & Quadrant HT* [2010] 1 WLR 363, [2009] EWCA Civ 587 and *R (McIntyre) v Gentoo Group Ltd* [2010] 2 P & CR DG6, [2010] EWHC 5 (Admin).

underlying disadvantages facing protected groups. The intended effect is that the decision will then be taken with the need to achieve the 'equality aims' well in mind.

The PSED applies in England, Wales and Scotland. There have (to date) been no amendments to the legislation, although paragraph 2 of Schedule 18 to the 2010 Act modifies the application of section 149 in the context of immigration enforcement, which is of little relevance to housing practitioners (except in accommodation challenges relating to support for migrants and asylum seekers).

1.3 The protected characteristics

Section 4 of the Equality Act 2010 lists nine protected characteristics, but the PSED only applies to only eight of them: marriage & civil partnership is excluded from section 149's protection. The relevant characteristics are therefore:

- age;
- disability;
- gender reassignment;
- pregnancy and maternity;
- race;
- religion or belief;
- sex;
- sexual orientation.

The relevant protected characteristics are also treated differently within section 149 itself. Sub-section (4) applies specifically to disability. The effect is that, when a public authority is complying with sub-section 3(b) in a disability case, it must take account of the person's disabilities. It is difficult to see how this would make a significant difference in practice, given the courts' repeated emphasis on the need for a 'sharp focus' on disability when complying with the PSED more generally. However, there may be room for public authorities to argue that some of the jurisprudence relating to disability is derived from sub-section (4), and is not, therefore, of more general application.

Apart from sub-section (4) – and although certain protected characteristics, in certain contexts, may call for greater attention – there is no formal 'hierarchy' of the PSED's protected characteristics[8]. In other words, while there is (strictly speaking) always a need to comply with the PSED, in many contexts a breach will simply be immaterial, but this is determined by the facts and not by the legislation itself. For example, it would probably be superfluous to insist on strict compliance with the PSED with regards to sex in a straightforward homelessness suitability case, in which sex plays no role on the facts of the case, but that is a matter of factual materiality rather than legislative technicality.

1.4 Process duty

The PSED is what is known as a 'process duty'[9]. A PSED challenge is an attack upon the way in which a decision has been reached, rather than a direct attack upon the decision itself. Of course, a litigant alleging a breach of the PSED will generally have the objective of seeing the relevant decision quashed, but the courts have repeatedly said that the PSED is 'not a duty to achieve a particular result'[10]. It cannot be over-emphasised

---

8 *Biden v Waverley BC* [2022] PTSR 1056, [2022] EWCA Civ 442, per Macur LJ at [54-56], on whether gender reassignment created a 'heightened duty'.

9 See, e.g., Fordham J's summary in *R (Rowley) v Minister for the Cabinet Office* [2022] 1 WLR 1189, [2021] EWHC 2108 (Admin), at [39].

10 *R (Hurley & Moore) v Secretary of State for Business, Education & Skills* [2012] HRLR 13, [2012] EWHC 201 (Admin), per Elias LJ at [76].

that a PSED point involves challenging the process, rather than the outcome, of a public authority's decision.

But that does not, of course, mean that the PSED is any less serious. As the Court of Appeal has noted: 'Public law is often concerned with the process by which a decision is taken and not with the substance of that decision' and its nature as a process duty does not diminish its importance. Instead, in common with other process duties, the PSED helps to ensure good, lawful public administration, and in particular 'helps to reassure members of the public, whatever their race or sex, that their interests have been properly taken into account before policies are formulated or brought into effect'[11].

1.5 Not a cause of action

Section 156 of the Equality Act 2010 specifically establishes that a breach of the PSED 'does not confer a cause of action at private law'[12]. This means that the PSED cannot be pleaded as a counter-claim in possession proceedings: it only works as a public law-type defence. It also means that – since it has been established that the County Court does not have jurisdiction to entertain discrimination challenges in statutory homelessness appeals[13] – the PSED could not be pleaded in any separate private law discrimination challenge brought against a local housing authority. In other words, for housing law purposes, the PSED may only form part of a defence to a possession claim, grounds for judicial review, or grounds of appeal in a statutory homelessness challenge.

---

11 *R (Bridges) v Chief Constable of South Wales Police* [2020] 1 WLR 5064, [2020] EWCA Civ 1058, per Sir Terence Etherton MR, Dame Victoria Sharp PQBD & Singh LJ at [176].

12 See also *Lalli v Spirita Housing* [2012] HLR 30, [2012] EWCA Civ 497, per Elias LJ at [43, 68].

13 *Adesotu v Lewisham LBC* [2019] 1 WLR 5637, [2019] EWCA Civ 1405.

1.6 A context-specific duty

In a social housing possession case, the Court of Appeal has pointed out that the PSED authorities are derived from many different types of challenge across all sorts of areas of public law: those authorities 'have to be taken in their context', and the duty's 'application will differ from case to case, depending upon the function being exercised and the facts of the case'[14]. It would be wrong, for example, for a court to conclude that a landlord considering an individual tenant's eviction should be required to comply with the PSED in exactly the same way as a minister deciding an issue of national policy. Practitioners should therefore be wary about borrowing one of the enormous number of dicta and statements of the law concerning the PSED, and seeking to cite in in a totally different context. Throughout this book, where propositions of law are stated, attempts have been made to ensure that a context-specific citation has been given.

1.7 Importance of the duty

Leading judges have stressed the importance of PSED-type duties as an instrument in guarding against discrimination[15]. The importance of the PSED is such that the United Kingdom government emphasises the duty in its submissions to international bodies[16]. Notionally, at least, the duty

---

[14] *Powell v Dacorum BC* [2019] HLR 21, [2019] EWCA Civ 23, per McCombe LJ at [44].

[15] *R (C) v Secretary of State for Justice* [2009] QB 657, [2008] EWCA Civ 882, per Buxton LJ at [49].

[16] See, e.g., *Concluding observations on the initial report of the United Kingdom of Great Britain and Northern Ireland: initial government response* at [139-114] (a response to the recommendations of the UN's Committee of the Rights of Persons with Disabilities); *United Nations Convention on the Elimination of All Forms of Discrimination against Women: United Kingdom's Eighth Periodic Report* at [4-6] (Amnesty International criticises the government's reliance on the PSED on the basis that the mechanism is too

is of the greatest importance – although there has been extensive judicial consideration of the materiality of established breaches of the PSED, as we shall see throughout this book.

weak (*United Kingdom: Submission to the United Nations Committee on the Elimination of Discrimination Against Women.*

CHAPTER TWO

POSSESSION PROCEEDINGS

2.1 A viable defence

The viability of the PSED as a defence to possession proceedings brought by social landlords was first established in 2011 in respect of a predecessor duty, the old section 49A of the Disability Discrimination Act 1995[17].

There was then a brief period in 2017-2018 when this was in some doubt: a High Court judge ruled that the tenant must have some private law right to remain in occupation in order to rely on the PSED[18]. But that decision was immediately reversed on appeal[19], and it is now well-established that the PSED operates as a form of public law defence[20]. It has been raised in both discretionary and mandatory grounds cases[21].

---

17 *Barnsley MBC v Norton* [2012] PTSR 54, [2011] EWCA Civ 834. At the time that the Court of Appeal handed down judgment in *Norton*, the new PSED come into force just a few months earlier. The judgment noted that the DDA duty had been replaced, and that the new PSED would now apply to the local authority landlord instead: per Lloyd LJ at [5, 22, 34-35, 41].

18 *Hertfordshire CC v Davies* [2017] 1 WLR 4395, [2017] EWHC 1488 (QB).

19 [2018] 1 WLR 4609, [2018] EWCA Civ 379, per Sharp LJ at [21, 23-28].

20 See e.g. *Patrick v London & Quadrant HT* [2020] HLR 3, [2019] EWHC 1263 (QB), approved by the Court of Appeal in *Forward v Aldwyck HG* [2020] 1 WLR 584, [2019] EWCA Civ 1334 (such approval noted by the Court of Appeal in *TM v Metropolitan HT* [2022] 1 WLR 2161, [2021] EWCA Civ 1890, per Nugee LJ at [17]).

21 As to the latter, see *Patrick v London & Quadrant HT* [2020] HLR 3, [2019] EWHC 1263 (QB) and *Guinness Partnership v England* (*Legal Action*, October 2019), both of which concerned 'absolute and mandatory' grounds.

While the PSED will often be pleaded alongside substantive discrimination defences, it is capable of operating independently, as a free-standing and complete defence. The Court of Appeal has dismissed a claim for possession on the sole basis of a breach of the PSED in a case where discrimination and all other lines of defence had failed[22].

There is often, though, a considerable overlap with discrimination defences, particularly where the defence is brought under section 35 of the Equality Act 2010. When a discrimination defence succeeds, there is very likely to have been a breach of the PSED as well: how can a landlord have had due regard to the need to eliminate discrimination when it is, itself, discriminating against the tenant by seeking their eviction? There is also Supreme Court authority in support of the proposition that a public authority that has failed to discharge its PSED is in no position to show that any discrimination is justified[23], so the PSED can often bolster a discrimination defence. But the point is not simply that the two defences can go hand-in-hand.

Instead, the important thing to note is that proper compliance with the PSED ought to prevent landlords from discriminating against tenants (by taking steps to evict them) in the first place. In one striking first instance case brought against a tenant on the basis of her disability-related conduct, the circuit judge dismissed the claim and awarded damages of £27,500 on the discrimination counterclaim. The judge said: 'a grasp by [the landlord] of these and the other dimensions of the public sector equality duty may have transformed the way in which the difficulties on Parkview Way were addressed [...] If ever there was a case in which the social housing provider needed to acknowledge, become familiar with and then discharge the public sector equality duty with vigour it was this one. From a very early stage is should have been obvious to [the landlord] that [the tenant's] condition, particularly if untreated and worsening,

---

22 *TM v Metropolitan HT* [2022] 1 WLR 2161, [2021] EWCA Civ 1890.

23 *R (Hussein) v Secretary of State for the Home Department* [2018] ACD 32, [2018] EWHC 213 (Admin), per Holman J at [57-58], considering *R (Coll) v Secretary of State for Justice* [2017] 1 WLR 2903, [2017] UKSC 40.

would need to be accommodated with reason and understanding by her neighbours and that it would itself need specialist expertise to address a situation with which its own staff had little or no experience'. He went on: 'The present proceedings should never have been brought'[24].

All local authority landlords are subject to the PSED because they are, inherently, public authorities. While the point has not yet been contested in a reported PSED possession dispute, most social landlords – depending on factors such as the size of their stock, receipt of public funds, and their level of cooperation with the local authority – are likely to be caught by the duty on the basis that they are exercising public functions[25].

2.2 When to comply

In theory – and as a matter of best practice – landlords must comply with the PSED right at the start of a case, when they are deciding whether or not to pursue an eviction.

That is because the courts have repeatedly emphasised that public authorities must comply with the PSED <u>before</u> a particular decision is reached. The Court of Appeal has explained that the purpose of the old Race Relations Act duty was to require public authorities to give 'advance consideration' to issues of discrimination[26], and – in another case – that

---

24 *Rosebery HA v Williams* (unrep.) [2021] 12 WLUK 464, per HHJ Luba KC at [135, 151, 168].

25 Equality Act 2010, section 149(2). See, e.g. *R (TRX) v Network Homes Ltd* [2022] EWHC 456 (Admin), applying *R (Weaver) v London & Quadrant HT* [2010] 1 WLR 363, [2009] EWCA Civ 587 and *R (McIntyre) v Gentoo Group Ltd* [2010] 2 P & CR DG6, [2010] EWHC 5 (Admin).

26 *R (Elias) v Secretary of State for Defence* [2006] 1 WLR CA, [2006] EWCA Civ 1293, per Arden LJ at [272-274]. This point in *Elias* has subsequently been applied in e.g: *R (Kaur & Shah) v Ealing LBC* [2008] EWHC 2062 (Admin) per Moses LJ at [23]; *R (C) v Secretary of State for Justice* [2008] EWHC 171 (Admin) per Muarice Kay LJ at [37, 39]; the appeal in *R (C)* [2009] QB 657, [2008] EWCA Civ 882, per Buxton LJ at [49]; *R (Brown)*

compliance must take place 'not as a rearguard action following a concluded decision but as an essential preliminary'[27]. Specifically in the housing possession context, a High Court judge has said that compliance with the PSED 'must be done with an open mind and not as a defensive "sweep-up"'[28]. Landlords should therefore not reach a decision as to whether to seek possession without having first complied with the PSED.

However, there are two important caveats to that principle. First, the PSED is a continuing duty[29]. This means that compliance does not take place once and for all, when the landlord is deciding whether or not it thinks the tenant ought to be evicted. Instead, the duty requires social landlords to comply with the duty at every stage of the proceedings.

Second, while the point may not be entirely settled, it appears that the effect of the Court of Appeal's decision in *TM v Metropolitan* is that a breach of the PSED at an early stage can in principle be 'remedied' by later compliance[30]. Where a landlord has complied with the duty late, that does not mean that there was never a breach: instead, it means that

---

v Secretary of State for Work & Pensions [2009] PTSR 1506, [2008] EWHC 3158 (Admin), per Scott Baker and Aikens LJJ at [88]; *R (Hurley & Moore) v Secretary of State for Business, Education & Skills* [2012] HRLR 13, [2012] EWHC 201 (Admin), per Elias LJ at [71-72]; and – perhaps most authoritatively – *Bracking v Secretary of State for Work & Pensions* [2014] EqLR 60, [2013] EWCA Civ 1345, per McCombe LJ at [26(4)].

27 *R (BAPIO Action Ltd) v Secretary of State for the Home Department* [2007] EWCA Civ 1139, per Sedley LJ at [3].

28 *Forward v Aldwyck HG* [2019] HLR 20, [2019] EWHC 24 (QB), per Cheema-Grubb J at [39] (her decision was upheld by the Court of Appeal).

29 *R (Brown) v Secretary of State for Work & Pensions* [2009] PTSR 1506, [2008] EWHC 3158 (Admin), per Scott Baker and Aikens LJJ at [95], applied in *Bracking v Secretary of State for Work & Pensions* [2014] EqLR 60, [2013] EWCA Civ 1345, per McCombe LJ at [26(5)(v)]. For application in the possession context, see *Patrick v London & Quadrant HT* [2020] HLR 3, [2019] EWHC 1263 (QB), per Turner J at [42(v)].

30 [2022] 1 WLR 2161, [2021] EWCA Civ 1890, per Nugee LJ at [43-47]. See also Green LJ at [62-64]. Strictly speaking, this point was decided *obiter*.

the initial breach may no longer have any continuing consequences, which will inform the court's decision as to whether to grant any remedy to the tenant in consequence of the landlord's breach.

However, social landlords would be best advised to comply with the PSED before they issue the claim: partly because this would achieve the statutory aim of ensuring that their decisions are informed by a 'full appraisal' of equality issues; partly because it may nip any substantive discrimination issues in the bud (as it should have in the *Rosebery* case cited in section 2.1 above); and partly because it would avoid complex and risky disputes about whether later attempts at compliance were an exercise in 'confirmation bias', which the courts may treat with greater scrutiny[31]. And the later the attempt, the more difficult it may be to satisfy the court that there has been compliance: as the Court of Appeal said of the risk of confirmation bias in *TM v Metropolitan*: 'this perhaps particularly so in the case of litigation, where costs have already been incurred and the incentive to pursue the proceedings to a successful conclusion can be very high'[32].

2.3 Triggering compliance

Plainly, there is no need for social landlords to comply with the PSED in every possession case. It will not always be relevant or necessary, so what is the threshold for triggering the duty? In a homelessness case, the Court of Appeal has framed the question as being: whether some feature of the evidence presents a real possibility that the person is disabled in a relevant sense[33]. As to what constitutes a 'relevant sense', see '2.9 Consequences

---

[31] Ibid. at [39, 65]. See also *R (Ward & Gullu) v Hillingdon LBC* [2019] PTSR 1738, [2019] EWCA Civ 692, per Lewison LJ at [76].

[32] [2022] 1 WLR 2161, [2021] EWCA Civ 1890, per Nugee LJ at [39.] See also Green LJ's comments at [65].

[33] *Pieretti v Enfield LBC* [2011] PTSR 565, [2010] EWCA Civ 1104, per Wilson LJ at [35]. While this statement of the law has been endorsed in the possession context in *Patrick v London & Quadrant HT* [2020] HLR 3, [2019] EWHC 1263 (QB), per Turner J at [42(iii)], it should be noted that

of breach' below. It appears that the PSED would be triggered if the occupier or any member of the household meets that test[34]. And, of course, disability is not the only protected characteristic that may be relevant (although it is by far the most common in the reported cases). But tenants or their representatives will probably need to take active steps to explain a more unusual PSED issue to the landlord, because the PSED generally only obliges decision-makers to consider 'obvious impacts on equality' and not 'every conceivable impact'[35].

It is worth noting that the threshold for 'disability' is low. Section 6 of the Equality Act 2010, read with section 212, has the effect that a person is under the protected characteristic of disability if they have a physical or mental impairment which has an adverse effect on their ability to carry out normal day-to-day activities, and the effect is more than minor or trivial. Thus the PSED has a very light trigger: an occupier must merely present a 'real possibility' of a condition that has a 'more than minimal' effect on their daily living, assuming that the disability is in some way relevant to the possession claim. However, the Court of Appeal has made the perhaps-obvious point that if the evidence has established that the tenant's condition does not constitute a disability, a PSED defence based on disability cannot succeed[36].

---

the Court of Appeal had previously cautioned (in another possession case, albeit where the tenant was not disabled) against 'wrenching that statement completely out of context' (*Swan HA v Gill* [2014] HLR 18, [2013] EWCA Civ 1556, per Lewison LJ at [41]).

34 In *Barnsley MBC v Norton* [2012] PTSR 54, [2011] EWCA Civ 834 it was the occupier's daughter, rather than the defendant himself, who was under a disability. See also *Guinness Partnership v England* (*Legal Action* October 2019), in which the landlord had failed to consider the impact of the eviction on the tenant's autistic son.

35 *R (Sheakh) v Lambeth LBC* [2022] PTSR 1315, [2022] EWCA Civ 457, per Sir Keith Lindblom SPT, Males & Laing LJJ at [15].

36 *Swan HA v Gill* [2014] HLR 18, [2013] EWCA Civ 1556.

There are three medical conditions that always constitute disabilities, regardless of severity: cancer, multiple sclerosis and HIV[37]. There are also a number of conditions which regulations exclude from the definition of disability. These include substance addiction, tendency to start fires, tendency to steal, tendency to commit physical or sexual abuse, exhibitionism and voyeurism[38]. There is also statutory guidance on the definition of disability, which contains some useful practical examples and case studies[39]. This guidance is particularly useful where there is an overlap between excluded conditions and other disabilities, for example where mental ill-health gives rise to substance misuse. Courts must take that guidance into account where it is relevant[40].

If it is unclear whether the PSED applies, or whether it is relevant, the duty itself may oblige landlords to carry out further inquiries to reach an answer, so that they make their decision from a properly-informed perspective[41]. This might, for example, involve seeking further medical evidence[42], or asking the tenant about the effects of their conditions, or the link between their conditions and the issue underlying the possession claim, or the likely impact of an eviction.

---

37 Equality Act 2010, schedule 1 para 6.

38 Equality Act 2010 (Disability) Regulations 2010, regs. 3-4.

39 'Equality Act 2010 Guidance: Guidance on matters to be taken into account in determining questions relating to the definition of disability', Office for Disability Issues.

40 Equality Act 2010, schedule 1 para 12. The guidance is issued pursuant to sub-section 6(5) of the Act.

41 *R (Hurley & Moore) v Secretary of State for Business, Education & Skills* [2012] HRLR 13, [2012] EWHC 201 (Admin) per Elias LJ at [89-90], endorsed in the possession context in *Patrick v London & Quadrant HT* [2020] HLR 3, [2019] EWHC 1263 (QB), per Turner J at [42(iii)]. See 'Inquiries and evidence gathering' under '2.5 Aspects of compliance' below.

42 See, e.g. *Forward v Aldwyck HG* [2020] 1 WLR 584, [2019] EWCA Civ 1334, per Longmore LJ at [12].

Where a social landlord has failed to comply with the PSED on its own initiative, or where the landlord did not know about an equality issue, or where the evidence has not alerted them of the need to comply, the tenant can also trigger the PSED by raising the relevant matters to the landlord at a later date[43]. This might be done, for example, by providing the landlord with medical or impact evidence, writing to the landlord explicitly raising the PSED, or pleading the PSED in a defence. The landlord would then be in breach from that point onwards until it complies, and faces the additional difficulty that any such compliance would necessarily be an *ex post facto* justification of a decision that has already been taken, which the courts may subject to greater scrutiny[44].

Failing that, and arising from the fact that the PSED is an ongoing duty, landlords need to re-comply when some feature of the case changes, or some new evidence emerges. In *TM v Metropolitan*, for example, the breach of the PSED took the form of failing to re-comply with the duty at a point when new medical evidence (which concerned both the tenant's capacity, and the impact of the court proceedings upon him) became available[45]. The Court of Appeal was highly critical of the consequences that this breach set into motion: 'This appeal amounts to a third level of judicial intervention. The costs incurred are significant, both to the public purse and in terms of court resources. […] An independent, objective, review by a fresh pair of eyes can bring a dispute to a swift solution avoiding hard-fought litigation. The failure to have

---

43 *R (Ward & Gullu) v Hillingdon LBC* [2019] PTSR 1738, [2019] EWCA Civ 692, per Lewison LJ at [72-74]. In the possession context, see *Patrick v London & Quadrant HT* [2020] HLR 3, [2019] EWHC 1263 (QB), per Turner J at [44]: 'I find that it was only upon receipt of the medical evidence that the Trust could sensibly be expected to engage with its PSED'.

44 Ibid. (*Ward & Gullu*) at [76]. See also e.g. *TM v Metropolitan HT* [2022] 1 WLR 2161, [2021] EWCA Civ 1890, per Nugee LJ at [39] and Green LJ at [65]. But see '2.4 Evidence; Tenant's evidence', below.

45 *TM v Metropolitan HT* [2022] 1 WLR 2161, [2021] EWCA Civ 1890, per Nugee LJ at [27, 64].

such a system in place has led in this case to the squandering of scarce resources far better deployed elsewhere'[46].

2.4 Evidence

Presumably – although it does not appear to have been tested in the possession context – section 136 of the Equality Act 2010 applies to PSED challenges in possession proceedings. This means that the landlord will bear the burden of proving that it has complied with the PSED, if there are facts from which the court could decide (in the absence of any other explanation) that the landlord has not complied. In other words, the burden of proof shifts to the landlord when there is a *prima facie* case of a non-compliance.

Landlords' evidence

While it is not a strict legal requirement of the PSED itself, the courts have repeatedly pointed out that keeping records of compliance is 'good practice' or an 'important evidential element in demonstrating the discharge of the duty'[47]. Whether or not such records are produced, there must at least be some evidence of what the landlord did to discharge the duty, which must go beyond mere generalities[48].

---

46 Ibid. per Green LJ at [67].

47 *R (Brown) v Secretary of State for Work & Pensions* [2009] PTSR 1506, [2008] EWHC 3158 (Admin), per Scott Baker and Aikens LJJ at [96]; *Bracking v Secretary of State for Work & Pensions* [2014] EqLR 60, [2013] EWCA Civ 1345, per McCombe LJ at [26(2)].

48 *R (Good Law Project) v Prime Minister* [2022] ACD 50, [2022] EWHC 298 (Admin), per Singh LJ at [112, 114, 116]. But cf. *Patrick v London & Quadrant HT* [2020] HLR 3, [2019] EWHC 1263 (QB), an earlier decision in the possession context, in which Turner J held that the landlord had shown compliance with the PSED by merely considering that medical evidence did not affect its decision.

A practice has developed among social landlords of demonstrating compliance through some form of written impact assessment. This dates back to the 'racial equality impact assessments' that used to be carried out to demonstrate compliance with the old Race Relations Act duty. But it should be emphasised that merely preparing an impact assessment is not, itself, compliance with the PSED. Such an assessment is only evidence, which records the steps that the decision-maker has taken when complying (or attempting to comply) with the duty. Indeed, it may be possible to comply with the duty without adducing a formal assessment[49] – and it is settled law that compliance with the PSED does not need to take any specific form[50] – although failing to carry out an impact assessment may be a high-risk approach for a landlord. And even where one is produced, the authorities demonstrate that tenants and judges are not obliged to take such documents at face-value, but the decision-maker may be called and cross-examined on the contents or adequacy of the assessment[51].

49 *Taylor v Slough BC* [2021] HLR 28, [2020] EWHC 3520 (Ch), per Zacaroli J at [46]. It may be difficult to reconcile Zacaroli J's approach to this evidential point with the Court of Appeal's earlier decision in *Luton CHT v Durdana* [2020] HLR 19, [2020] EWCA Civ 445, in which Patten LJ appeared to accept at [21] that the PSED would, in practice, require the landlord to carry out an assessment. But note that Zacaroli J's 'reasoning and conclusion' regarding another point – retrospective compliance – were endorsed by the Court of Appeal in *TM v Metropolitan HT* [2022] 1 WLR 2161, [2021] EWCA Civ 1890, per Nugee LJ at [47]. See also the discussion of late evidence in the next sub-section, below.

50 *R (Sheakh) v Lambeth LBC* [2022] PTSR 1315, [2022] EWCA Civ 457, per Sir Keith Lindblom SPT, Males & Laing LJJ at [10].

51 See, e.g., *Powell v Dacorum BC* [2019] HLR 21, [2019] EWCA Civ 23; *Guinness Partnership v England* (*Legal Action* October 2019); *Forward v Aldwyck HG* [2020] 1 WLR 584, [2019] EWCA Civ 1334; *Luton CHT v Durdana* [2020] HLR 19, [2020] EWCA Civ 445; *TM v Metropolitan HT* [2022] 1 WLR 2161, [2021] EWCA Civ 1890; *Rosebery HA v Williams* (Unrep.) [2021] 12 WLUK 464. But cf *Patrick v London & Quadrant HT* [2020] HLR 3, [2019] EWHC 1263 (QB): in that case the first-instance judge made a possession order summarily, although he had been prepared to

The authorities also show examples of social landlords trying to evidence compliance with the PSED by adducing 'proportionality assessments'. 'Proportionality' is a facet of discrimination law (under both the Equality Act 2010 and European human rights law), so it is plainly of some relevance to the PSED. But the courts have been clear that compliance with the PSED is distinct from – and requires more than – an assessment of the proportionality of evicting the tenant[52]. A proportionality assessment by itself is unlikely to be sufficient.

Ultimately, written assessments can only take landlords so far, and the real decision-making process will often only become clear when the landlord's witness gives live evidence. Where the assessment is challenged it may well be in the interests of fairness for the decision-maker to be called as a witness because the PSED falls upon the decision-maker personally[53], and cross-examination can be an informative and fruitful exercise. In *Luton CHT v Durdana*, for example, the witness who had prepared the 'Equality Act Review' explained to the trial judge that she had never read section 149, and had no idea what the PSED comprised of[54]. In *Forward v Aldwyck* the decision-maker conceded that she had not obtained evidence about the impact of a known disability, and had not

---

find (for the sake of argument) that the landlord was in breach, so there was no need to hear evidence on the point (per Turner J at [22-23, 43]). Similarly, in *Taylor v Slough BC* [2021] HLR 28, [2020] EWHC 3520 (Ch) the decision-maker did not give evidence, but it was common ground that she had initially breached the PSED (per Zacaroli J at [8, 19, 31]).

52 *Luton CHT v Durdana* [2020] HLR 19, [2020] EWCA Civ 445, per Patten LJ at [27]; *Forward v Aldwyck HG* [2019] HLR 20, [2019] EWHC 24 (QB), per Cheema-Grubb J at [39] (her decision was upheld by the Court of Appeal).

53 *Bracking v Secretary of State for Work & Pensions* [2014] EqLR 60, [2013] EWCA Civ 1345, per McCombe LJ at [26(3)]. See also *R (Nur) v Birmingham CC (no.1)* [2021] HLR 23, [2021] EWHC 3526 (Admin.) per David Lock QC at [49]: evidence from a member of staff about why she believed the public authority might have taken a particular approach did not demonstrate compliance with the PSED.

54 [2020] HLR 19, [2020] EWCA Civ 445, per Patten LJ at [11].

prepared her assessment with an open mind[55]. In *TM v Metropolitan* the assessment had been prepared by another agency entirely, and had in fact misinformed the landlord's decision-maker as to the severity of the tenant's anti-social behaviour[56]. In *Rosebery HA v Williams* the witness 'fully acknowledged that he did not know of the terms of section 149 and was not familiar with the [PSED]'[57].

Nevertheless, impact assessments are now effectively a prerequisite in many disability cases, and their preparation should be taken very seriously even if the landlord intends to call a live witness at trial. In fact, cases like *Durdana, Forward, TM* and *Williams* only emphasise this point: when impact assessments are carried out in a genuinely rigourous, sympathetic and open-minded way from the outset, there is a far smaller risk of embarrassing and expensive incidents in cross-examination.

Tenants' evidence

As far as the tenant's evidence is concerned, and notwithstanding that the duty of inquiry is on the landlord, it is clear that defendants will need to adduce something to show that the equality issue is genuine and relevant. In *Forward v Aldwyck*, for example, the tenant failed to satisfy the trial judge that he had a mental impairment. More importantly, the underlying factual thrust of the tenant's case – that he was a vulnerable person who was the victim of a 'cuckooing' operation in his home – was rejected by the trial judge. This badly undermined his case on the materiality of a breach of the PSED (which, as established, related to a physical condition, rather than the mental impairment on which his case relied)[58]. Tenants' representatives should take care to ensure that the best possible factual and medical evidence is available, and should certainly not rely on the fact that the duty of inquiry is – strictly speaking – on the

55 [2020] 1 WLR 584, [2019] EWCA Civ 1334, per Longmore LJ at [12].

56 [2022] 1 WLR 2161, [2021] EWCA Civ 1890, per Nugee LJ at [26(4)-)5)].

57 (Unrep.) [2021] 12 WLUK 464, per HHJ Luba KC at [135].

58 [2020] 1 WLR 584, [2019] EWCA Civ 1334, per Longmore LJ at [13, 15, 17, 38-40].

landlord. By the time of the trial, the tenant's evidence should be in the form of proper witness statements, exhibits, and possibly part-35-compliant expert evidence. For the purposes of obtaining directions to trial, a fully pleaded and signed defence setting out the tenant's factual case, together with some medical evidence establishing disability, ought to be sufficient in most cases.

The effect of late medical evidence is a vexed question. In *TM v Metropolitan*, as noted under '2.3 Triggering compliance' above, the Court of Appeal was highly critical of the landlord's failure to carry out a proper PSED assessment when new medical evidence emerged while proceedings were in train, and emphasised the risk of 'confirmation bias' in complying with the PSED in circumstances where medical evidence post-dated the decision to evict. In that case, an expert's report had been served a few days before the first possession hearing[59]. But in *Patrick v London & Quadrant*, the tenant had – very similarly – provided medical evidence just before a CPR Part 55 possession hearing, and the High Court suggested that 'eleventh hour' medical evidence might actually merit a less thorough exercise than the PSED would ordinarily require[60]: the landlord in that case was held to have complied with its PSED by merely taking the view that the medical evidence did not cast doubt on the appropriateness of its decision to seek possession. So on the one hand, the Court of Appeal in *TM* suggested that *ex post facto* PSED assessments (which are necessarily the case where medical evidence is provided late) might be subjected to equal or even greater scrutiny to guard against confirmation bias[61], while on the other, the High Court held in *Patrick*

---

59 [2022] 1 WLR 2161, [2021] EWCA Civ 1890, per Nugee LJ at [27].

60 [2020] HLR 3, [2019] EWHC 1263 (QB), per Turner J at [42(vi), 44].

61 *TM v Metropolitan HT* [2022] 1 WLR 2161, [2021] EWCA Civ 1890, per Nugee LJ at [39] and Green LJ at [65]. See also *R (Ward & Gullu) v Hillingdon LBC* [2019] PTSR 1738, [2019] EWCA Civ 692, per Lewison LJ at [76]. *Ward & Gullu* was handed down after *Patrick* was heard but before judgment was given (and there may therefore be an argument that *Patrick* is not authoritative). *TM* also post-dated *Patrick* by more than two years. See also *R (Rowley) v Minister for the Cabinet Office* [2022] 1 WLR 1189, [2021] EWHC 2108 (Admin): a later case, in which another High

that a much less formal standard of compliance can be tolerated in late evidence cases.

It is difficult to know what to make of this, except that judges' approaches will be fact-specific. *TM* was a very sympathetic case, in which the disability was undoubted and serious (the tenant lived in a form of care home, and the expert report established that he lacked capacity) and the landlord had initially done its best to comply with the PSED; whereas the medical evidence in *Patrick* was less compelling, the PSED did not even arise until the late evidence was produced, and the judge was particularly concerned about the ongoing impact on the tenant's neighbour. But the question about the standard of scrutiny to be applied in late evidence cases appears to be unsettled.

Tenants' lawyers should lose no time, and should (despite the duty being ostensibly on the landlord to make inquiries) obtain medical evidence as soon as possible. Certainly, they should not delay for tactical reasons, and a clear lesson from *Patrick* is that the lateness of any medical evidence should be well-explained. But equally, where medical evidence is served late, landlords would be well-advised to carry out a proper, open-minded and conscientious PSED exercise. The decision in *Patrick*, if it remains good law, may be less reliable than it once was, and the courts may no longer be satisfied with poor-quality or badly-evidenced assessments prepared at the door of the court.

Court judge (Fordham J) held in a different context that 'the standards of scrutiny remain the same' even where a PSED assessment carried out 'at the door of the court' (at [43]); and *Luton CHT v Durdana* [2020] HLR 19, [2020] EWCA Civ 445 (in which Patten LJ appeared to accept at [21] that the PSED would, in practice, require the landlord to carry out a proper assessment when it becomes aware of a relevant disability).

2.5 Aspects of compliance

The point of the PSED is that landlords should have a moment of frank and serious reflection. No matter what has led the landlord to this point, in a PSED case the tenant who they are considering evicting is likely to face structural disadvantage – whether due to disability, race, gender, sexuality, or a combination of matters – and to deprive them of their home is often extremely serious. The PSED requires landlords to face up to the adverse circumstances facing their tenants, and to reach their decisions in full consciousness of those circumstances.

But a PSED defence is a challenge to the decision-making process, not the outcome[62]. A tenant pleading the PSED is only ever saying 'the landlord has not thought about this carefully enough', rather than 'the landlord has reached the wrong decision'. This, though, does not diminish the importance of the duty[63].

Like many nebulous legal concepts, compliance with the PSED has something of the 'elephant test' about it: it is difficult to describe by putting into words, but you know it when you see it. Thankfully for practitioners, though, the courts have identified a number of helpfully discrete aspects of compliance with the duty.

<u>The statutory criteria</u>

The starting point for complying with the PSED is the words of the statute itself. Despite the many judicial statements summarising the spirit and purpose of the PSED, there is no better guide for housing officers (or tenants or judges scrutinising PSED compliance) than the primary legislation. Indeed, the courts have explicitly said that that compliance means showing a 'proper and conscientious focus on the statutory

---

62 See, e.g. *R (Rowley) v Minister for the Cabinet Office* [2022] 1 WLR 1189, [2021] EWHC 2108 (Admin), per Fordham J at [39].

63 *R (Bridges) v Chief Constable of South Wales Police* [2020] 1 WLR 5064, [2020] EWCA Civ 1058, per Sir Terence Etherton MR, Dame Victoria Sharp PQBD & Singh LJ at [176].

criteria'[64], that judicial decisions describing the PSED are merely 'glosses' which 'are no substitute for the statute'[65], and that there is a difference between loose, general regard to equality issues more broadly (which does not amount to compliance with the PSED) and having specific regard to the section 149 criteria (which does)[66].

Section 149 therefore provides an essential checklist. Both parties should ensure that that the landlord demonstrated a proper, conscientious focus on:

- The possibility that there has been discrimination, harassment (in the strict statutory sense, i.e. 'unwanted conduct' relevant to a protected characteristic)[67], victimisation (also in the strict statutory sense, i.e. subjecting someone to a detriment in

---

[64] *Bracking v Secretary of State for Work & Pensions* [2014] EqLR 60, [2013] EWCA Civ 1345, per McCombe LJ at [26(8)(i)], citing Elias LJ in *Hurley & Moore* at [78].

[65] *R (Sheakh) v Lambeth LBC* [2022] PTSR 1315, [2022] EWCA Civ 457, per Sir Keith Lindblom SPT, Males & Laing LJJ at [13].

[66] *R (Meaney) v Harlow DC* (unrep.) [2009] EWHC 559 (Admin) per Davis J at [84], cited with approval in *R (Sheakh) v Lambeth LBC* [2022] PTSR 1315, [2022] EWCA Civ 457, per Sir Keith Lindblom SPT, Males & Laing LJJ at [12]. See also *R (MA) v Secretary of State for Work & Pensions* [2016] 1 WLR 4550, [2016] UKSC 58, per Lord Toulson at [68].

[67] Equality Act 2010, section 26. It is not uncommon for housing officers in anti-social behaviour cases to misunderstand references to 'harassment' when the word is included in *pro forma* impact assessments, and to assume that the term refers to general nuisance behaviour carried out by the tenants themselves (see e.g. *Patrick v London & Quadrant HT* [2020] HLR 3, [2019] EWHC 1263 (QB), per Turner J at [45]). This is wrong: the 'equality aim' is the elimination of statutory harassment, for example homophobic taunting, unwelcome sexualised remarks, transphobic comments, unwanted 'where are you really from' conversations regarding race and ethnicity, etc., and it is important for landlords to focus on any such conduct that may have been directed towards the tenant.

retaliation for relying on their Equality Act protections[68]), and/or other prohibited conduct such as a failure to make reasonable adjustments[69];

- The need to advance equality of opportunity, which includes having regard to the need to:
    - Remove or minimise disadvantages that people with protected characteristics face;
    - Take steps to meet the different needs of people with protected characteristics;
    - Encourage people with protected characteristics to participate in public life and societal activity;
- The need to foster good relations, which includes having regard to the need to:
    - Tackle prejudice;
    - Promote understanding;
- The particular needs of people with disabilities; and
- Whether it may be appropriate to treat tenants with protected characteristics more favourably than others.

In essence, and where appropriate, compliance with the PSED involves considering those matters 'in substance, with rigour and with an open

[68] Equality Act 2010, section 27.

[69] Breach of the reasonable adjustment duty is, strictly speaking, a form of discrimination rather than 'any other conduct': Equality Act 2010, section 21(2).

mind'[70]. The Court of Appeal has also expressed the duty in the possession context as simply requiring an 'open-minded conscientious inquiry'[71].

'Due' regard & weight

Those statutory matters require 'due' regard. The courts have interpreted this as meaning the degree of regard that is 'appropriate in all the circumstances'[72]. The Supreme Court has expressed its regret that 'this was not a particularly helpful guide', but nevertheless endorsed the point, which (they said) was unavoidable because of Parliament's inclusion of the word 'due' in the statute. Lord Neuberger PSC concluded: 'I do not think it is possible to be more precise or prescriptive, given that the weight and extent of the duty are highly fact-sensitive and dependent on individual judgment'[73].

What this means in practice is that the attention that landlords must pay to the PSED will be different in virtually every case. In certain respects this is obvious. Given that most people are under the protected characteristic of sex[74], and despite the systemic misogyny that prevails in

---

70 *Patrick v London & Quadrant HT* [2020] HLR 3, [2019] EWHC 1263 (QB), per Turner J at [42(iv)].

71 *Luton CHT v Durdana* [2020] HLR 19, [2020] EWCA Civ 445, per Patten LJ at [27].

72 *Pieretti v Enfield LBC* [2011] PTSR 565, [2010] EWCA Civ 1104, per Wilson LJ at [33]. For an application in the possession context, see *Luton CHT v Durdana* [2020] HLR 19, [2020] EWCA Civ 445, per Patten LJ at [17-18].

73 *Hotak v Southwark LBC* [2016] AC 811, [2015] UKSC 30, per Lord Neuberger at [74].

74 Defined in section 11(a) of the Equality Act 2010 as 'a reference to a man or a woman', which necessarily means that non-binary and some intersex people are excluded from that protected characteristic. Non-binary genders are not currently recognised in UK law (see Fairbarn et all, 'Non-binary gender recognition: law and policy', House of Commons Library Research Briefing, 31st March 2022).

society, it would probably be foolhardy to run a defence arguing that landlords need to show a sharp focus on the need to minimise sex inequality in every case where the tenant happens to be a woman. Whereas at the other end of the scale there are cases where a characteristic such as disability is intimately bound-up with the reason for seeking possession, or where the tenant would need specialised accommodation if evicted, and landlords will need to pay very close attention indeed to the PSED. Lord Neuberger is, of course, right to say that what is 'due' is highly fact-sensitive, and it can be difficult to predict the approach that the courts may take in any given case.

Importantly for present purposes, in *Luton CHT v Durdana* the Court of Appeal emphasised the point that the PSED does not require public authorities to actually promote the equality aims, but merely to have regard to the need to promote them, and pointed out that this distinction is important[75]. On that basis the PSED in the possession context might be described as a fairly weak obligation: what is 'due' might not actually be very much. Set against that, though, various cases show that – where appropriate – the courts will dismiss possession claims on the basis that the landlord has not paid close enough attention to the statutory criteria; that in fact a great deal more had been 'due' from the landlord[76]. There is no getting around the fact that the PSED really is a very case-specific issue.

This is clear from the appeal cases in which different judges have dramatically reversed outcomes even when looking at the same facts. In a high-profile challenge to the introduction to automated facial recognition software in South Wales, a Divisional Court (Haddon-Cave LJ and Swift J) said that there was an 'air of unreality' about the PSED ground and dismissed the claim. A notable constitution of the Court of

75 [2020] HLR 19, [2020] EWCA Civ 445, per Patten LJ at [17], citing with approval *R (Baker) v Secretary of State for Communities & Local Government* [2009] PTSR 809, [2008] EWCA Civ 141 per Dyson LJ at [31].

76 See *Guinness Partnership v England* (*Legal Action* October 2019); *TM v Metropolitan HT* [2022] 1 WLR 2161, [2021] EWCA Civ 1890; *Rosebery HA v Williams* (unrep.) [2021] 12 WLUK 464.

Appeal (Sir Terence Etherton MR, Dame Victoria Sharp PQBD and Singh LJ) reversed them, saying: 'On the contrary, it seems to raise a serious issue of public concern'[77]. More familiar to housing practitioners will be *TM v Metropolitan* in which the High Court (Johnson J) refused to interfere with the trial judge's order on the basis that compliance with the PSED would have made no difference and that seeking possession was the 'right' decision, whereas the Court of Appeal not only allowed the appeal but dismissed the underlying claim entirely[78]. This degree of judicial unpredictability is, of course, a serious practical problem for social housing lawyers and their clients.

What is clear, though, is that it is for the landlord and not for the court to decide how much weight to give to the statutory criteria. As long as there has been 'proper and conscientious focus', the court cannot interfere with the decision 'simply because it would have given greater weight to the equality implications of the decision than did the decision maker'[79]. The battleground, therefore, is usually going to be whether the landlord's PSED exercise was so bad that it actually amounted to a failure to comply with the duty, rather than whether the landlord merely should have paid more attention to one aspect or another. This is a narrow distinction, but it can be an important one.

---

77 *R (Bridges) v Chief Constable of South Wales Police* [2020] 1 WLR 5064, [2020] EWCA Civ 1058 at [173].

78 [2022] 1 WLR 2161, [2021] EWCA Civ 1890. The High Court decision is (unrep.) [2020] EWHC 311 (QB).

79 *Luton CHT v Durdana* [2020] HLR 19, [2020] EWCA Civ 445, per Patten LJ at [22], applying *R (Hurley & Moore) v Secretary of State for Business, Education & Skills* [2012] HRLR 13, [2012] EWHC 201 (Admin) per Elias LJ at [78]. See also the High Court's guidance in *Patrick v London & Quadrant HT* [2020] HLR 3, [2019] EWHC 1263 (QB), per Turner J at [42(viii)].

Impact of the eviction

While not expressly set out in section 149 itself, the courts have established that assessing the impact of an eviction is an essential part of the PSED in possession proceedings. This stems from the more general PSED case law about the need to assess the impact of any given policy or decision[80], but the point has been authoritatively applied in the possession context[81]. Perhaps the most useful statement of the law is in *Hurley & Moore*, where Elias LJ said: 'In short, the decision maker must be clear precisely what the equality implications are when he puts them in the balance, and he must recognise the desirability of achieving them'[82].

What is the impact of an eviction likely to be? Each household will supply their own particulars. Have they experienced homelessness in the past? Is there a medical condition that would be exacerbated by an eviction? Do they have caring obligations? Are they at risk of domestic abuse? Do they have a history of disability-related substance dependency? The point of the PSED is, partly, to force landlords to reflect, very frankly, on the impact that a possession order would have on the particular tenant who has been brought before the court. This necessarily involves identifying what the impact is likely to be.

But there may also be more structural aspects to consider. The authorities – particularly in broader policy challenges – show that the PSED is in no

80 See, e.g. *Bracking v Secretary of State for Work & Pensions* [2014] EqLR 60, [2013] EWCA Civ 1345, per McCombe LJ at [26(4)]; *R (Bridges) v Chief Constable of South Wales Police* [2020] 1 WLR 5064, [2020] EWCA Civ 1058, per Sir Terence Etherton MR, Dame Victoria Sharp PQBD & Singh LJ at [175(6)]; *R (Rowley) v Minister for the Cabinet Office* [2022] 1 WLR 1189, [2021] EWHC 2108 (Admin), at [43].

81 *Luton CHT v Durdana* [2020] HLR 19, [2020] EWCA Civ 445, per Patten LJ at [21-22].

82 [2012] HRLR 13, [2012] EWHC 201 (Admin) at [78], applied in the possession context in *Luton CHT v Durdana* [2020] HLR 19, [2020] EWCA Civ 445, per Patten LJ at [22].

small part concerned with the general underlying disadvantages that protected groups face. For example, people under the protected characteristics of disability and race tend to face much worse housing outcomes in the private and social rented sectors. Although – lamentably – the government does not keep statistics, there is strong anecdotal evidence of an overlap between mental ill-health and landlords taking anti-social behaviour enforcement action[83]. The claimant landlord's own data may well bear this out, and there is an argument that the PSED obliges them to record and reflect on that data when deciding whether to evict a tenant with a psychiatric disability for anti-social behaviour[84]. Similarly, academic research shows that people from Black and minoritised racial backgrounds are significantly more likely to face both homelessness and discrimination by landlords[85]. A breach of the PSED consisting of a failure to consider sorts of structural issues has not yet appeared in the reported possession cases, but in appropriate circumstances it may be important to highlight the unacceptably divergent housing outcomes that different groups could expect to face if evicted.

Impact of a disability

In disability cases, as well as assessing the impact of an eviction on the household, the other side of the coin is that the PSED requires landlords to assess the impact that the disability has had (or will have) in circumstances of the case. This is clear from the statute itself: sub-section

83 See, e.g., Maeve McClenaghan, 'Sent to jail for feeding the pigeons: the broken system of antisocial behaviour laws', Bureau of Investigative Journalism, 21st August 2022.

84 See, by analogy, examples from the allocations field: *R (Nur) v Birmingham CC (no.2)* [2021] HLR 41, [2020] EWHC 1138 (Admin), per David Lock QC at [13, 28]; *R (H) v Ealing LBC (EHRC intervening)* [2018] PTSR 541, [2017] EWCA Civ 1127, per Sir Terence Etherton MR at [115].

85 Glen Bramley et al., 'Homelessness Amongst Black and Minoritised Ethnic Communities in the UK', Heriot Watt University, November 2022.

149(4) requires public authorities to take: 'in particular, steps to take account of disabled persons' disabilities'.

Thus, in *Durdana*, the Court of Appeal upheld the trial judge's determination that there had been a breach of the PSED in that the landlord 'had not taken into account the likely effect of the disabilities of the respondent and [her disabled daughter] in relation to their proposed eviction from the Premises'[86]. How would a disabled tenant fare if evicted? How, precisely, would the disability factor into that?

At the same, it may also be important to focus sharply on the impact that a disability has had on the landlord's decision to evict. Because the PSED is designed to encourage landlords to eliminate discrimination, there will be many cases in which the landlord will be required to consider whether they are themselves discriminating against the tenant by taking steps to evict them[87]. In cases of potential indirect discrimination under section 19 of the Equality Act 201, or discrimination arising from disability under section 15, questions are likely to arise as to the connection between the disability and the decision to evict. Where, for example, the landlord produces an impact assessment that claims to have focused sharply on the need to eliminate discrimination, but which nonetheless disputes, underplays or fails to consider whether the tenant's conduct 'arises from' their disability, the evidence will ring hollow[88].

Defining & acknowledging disability

In disability cases, landlords will often need (at the very least) to acknowledge that the tenant or occupier is under a disability. In one County Court case, for example, the claim was dismissed when the landlord had 'repeatedly' breached the PSED: 'The impact assessment had rejected the medical evidence concerning [the tenant's] mental health

86 *Luton CHT v Durdana* [2020] HLR 19, [2020] EWCA Civ 445, per Patten LJ at [26]; see also *Rosebery HA v Williams* (unrep.) [2021] 12 WLUK 464.

87 Section 35 of the Equality Act 2010 deems 'evicting [the occupier] (or taking steps to secure [their] eviction)' as capable of being an act of discrimination.

88 See e.g. *Rosebery HA v Williams* (unrep.) [2021] 12 WLUK 464.

without giving any reasons for doing so. The most recent assessment had only concluded that [the tenant] and her son might be disabled when the evidence conclusively pointed to them being disabled'[89] (original emphasis). If a tenant is caught by a relevant protected characteristic, there is simply no point from shying away from the fact, particularly since the Supreme Court has held (in another housing law context) that the PSED requires public authorities to 'focus very sharply' on whether and to what extent the person has a disability[90].

In a homelessness case, the Court of Appeal found a breach of the PSED where the local authority's assessment had 'down-graded' the symptoms of the applicant's disability, instead of acknowledging the effects of his medical condition[91]. It is important to be frank rather than dismissive.

Of course, in disability cases, proper compliance with the PSED probably requires the landlord get the legal definition of disability right[92]. As set out at '2.3 Triggering compliance' above, disability is a low threshold, and this can take housing officers by surprise. Landlords would be well-

---

89 *Guinness Partnership v England* (*Legal Action* October 2019).

90 *Hotak v Southwark LBC* [2016] AC 811, [2015] UKSC 30, per Lord Neuberger PSC at [78].

91 *Kannan v Newham LBC* [2019] HLR 22, [2019] EWCA Civ 57, per Lewison LJ at [21].

92 Cf. two homelessness authorities in which the Court of Appeal held that compliance with the PSED does not require an explicit or correct legal definition of disability to be set out: *Hackeny LBC v Haque* [2017] PTSR 769, [2017] EWCA Civ 4, per Briggs LJ at [49-50]; *McMahon v Watford BC* [2020] PTSR 1217, [2020] EWCA Civ 497, at [62]. See also [76-77] and [83-85]. In those cases, however, there was a close elision between the statutory homelessness question that the local authority was deciding and the requirements of the PSED, and the review decisions effectively treated the applicants as if they were under the protected characteristic. In an allocations case, it was a breach of the PSED for a local authority to use its own non-statutory definition of disability, and to fail to inquire into the effects of doing so: *R (H) v Ealing LBC (EHRC intervening)* [2018] PTSR 541, [2017] EWCA Civ 1127, per Sir Terence Etherton MR at [115].

advised to look at the statutory guidance carefully, and to ensure that their staff come to trial prepared to defend any assessment that purports to decide whether or not the tenant is protected by the PSED.

Open-mindedness

This is perhaps one of the most difficult and elusive aspects of the duty. Time and again, the courts have emphasised the need for open-mindedness when complying with the PSED[93]. However, particularly in possession proceedings, compliance with the PSED will take place in the context of the landlord trying to demonstrate to the court that its decision to evict the tenant is justified. It can be very difficult to demonstrate both open-mindedness and a firm, well-justified decision at the same time.

In general, the court's assessment of that exercise will boil down to the quality of the evidence. In *TM v Metropolitan*, for example, the trial judge and both appeal courts were full of praise for the compassionate, sympathetic conduct of Metropolitan's witness. Despite his ultimate failure to carry out a new assessment in the course of the litigation, it was clear that he had been open-minded whenever he had complied with the duty. In other cases, such as *Durdana*, the judgments describe the evidence much less effusively. A great deal will turn on the documentary and witness evidence, and the surrounding facts.

In *Forward v Aldwyck*, for example, the witness admitted in evidence that she had not been open-minded[94]. In a first instance case, a PSED assessment failed to consider evidence that supported the tenant's own case that she was being bullied by other tenants, and that this was the underlying cause of her anti-social behaviour[95].

---

93 In the possession context see, e.g. *Luton CHT v Durdana* [2020] HLR 19, [2020] EWCA Civ 445, per Patten LJ at [27]; *Patrick v London & Quadrant HT* [2020] HLR 3, [2019] EWHC 1263 (QB), per Turner J at [42(iv)].

94 [2020] 1 WLR 584, [2019] EWCA Civ 1334, per Longmore LJ at [12].

95 *Guinness Partnership v England* (*Legal Action*, October 2019).

Ultimately, open-minded compliance with the PSED involves balancing the factors in favour of an eviction with the equality issues and personal circumstances of the tenant. In evidencing that, it is important not to dodge the question, or to under-play the factors in the tenant's favour. Landlords must grasp the nettle, or they may face difficult and potentially costly consequences if a failure to be open-minded is established. In *Durdana*, for example, the Court of Appeal noted that: 'Under the heading "What issues are arising as a consequence of the tenant's disability?" Ms Wilson has summarised the circumstances in which the respondent and her family came to be granted the tenancy but says nothing about the effect of an eviction on their disabilities'[96]. The landlord had fallen into the easy trap of using the PSED to shore-up its case, rather than facing up to the fact that it was seeking to evict a disabled child and her disabled mother.

That is not to say that landlords are forbidden from citing the factors in favour of an eviction when complying with the PSED. On the contrary, the law is clear that a PSED assessment may involve consideration of 'countervailing factors' such as 'the impact which the disabled person's behaviour, in so far as is material to the decision in question, is having upon others (e.g. through drug dealing or other anti-social behaviour)'[97]. But the PSED is not an opportunity to twist the knife. Instead, landlords will be expected to show 'reason and understanding'[98].

---

[96] [2020] HLR 19, [2020] EWCA Civ 445, per Patten LJ at [14].

[97] *Patrick v London & Quadrant HT* [2020] HLR 3, [2019] EWHC 1263 (QB), per Turner J at [42(ii)].

[98] *Rosebery HA v Williams* (unrep.) [2021] 12 12 WLUK 464, per HHJ Luba KC at [151].

Not a 'box-ticking' exercise

The authorities repeatedly emphasise that the PSED is not an exercise in box-ticking[99]. The difficulty with possession proceedings, and the frequent use of *pro forma* impact assessments, is that there are often literal boxes to tick. At worst, landlords will merely fill in these forms and either fail to engage properly with the facts of the case, or (as in *Durdana*) use the PSED exercise as an opportunity to bolster their own decision by emphasising their own case and overlooking the tenant's.

There is nothing inherently wrong with *pro forma* impact assessment forms. A form or guidance document that explains the low threshold for establishing disability, directs the decision-maker towards the relevant questions and encourages them to seek more evidence can, in fact, be an excellent way of focusing the mind and ensuring compliance. But the courts will be alert to landlords who reduce compliance to a mere box-ticking exercise.

Considering all of the occupiers

The PSED can arise if any member of the household, and not just the tenants themselves, are under protected characteristics. This tends to happen in the case of children with disabilities[100], but there is no reason in principle why any occupier, or any protected characteristic, would not be relevant.

---

99 In the possession context see, e.g. *Patrick v London & Quadrant HT* [2020] HLR 3, [2019] EWHC 1263 (QB), per Turner J at [42(iv)].

100 *Barnsley MBC v Norton* [2012] PTSR 54, [2011] EWCA Civ 834; *Guinness Partnership v England* (*Legal Action* October 2019).

Avoiding confirmation bias

Judges will be alert to the possibility that the PSED assessment 'was produced with an "agenda", or that the writer was reasoning backwards from a chosen policy position being defended before a Court'[101]. In *TM v Metropolitan* the Court of Appeal said: 'there is an obvious danger of confirmation bias whenever a decision-maker carries out an assessment in relation to a decision that has already been made, rather than in advance; and this is perhaps particularly so in the case of litigation, when costs have already been incurred and the incentive to C pursue the proceedings to a successful conclusion can be very high'[102].

In practical terms, this overlaps with showing 'open-mindedness': it is a matter of evidence. The more frank and compassionate a landlord can be, the greater the chances that the court will accept that the need to achieve the equality aims has been borne well in mind.

Complying inadvertently

It has been established in other contexts that it is possible for a decision-maker to comply with the PSED even if they did not know that the duty existed[103]. Thus, in *Durdana*, the landlord argued that it had complied with the PSED even though its witness had admitted that she 'did not know what s.149 provided or what the PSED comprised of; and had not previously considered the PSED in relation to these proceedings'. The Court of Appeal held, though, that in the possession context: 'Although it is theoretically possible for the duty to be complied with in ignorance of what it consists of, such cases are likely to be rare and this is not one of them'[104].

---

101 *R (Rowley) v Minister for the Cabinet Office* [2022] 1 WLR 1189, [2021] EWHC 2108 (Admin), per Fordham J at [43].

102 [2022] 1 WLR 2161, [2021] EWCA Civ 1890, per Nugee LJ at [39].

103 *Hotak v Southwark LBC* [2016] AC 811, [2015] UKSC 30, per Lord Neuberger PSC at [79].

104 [2020] HLR 19, [2020] EWCA Civ 445, per Patten LJ at [11, 26].

In practice, it should be relatively easy to spot a conscientious landlord, who has given frank and open-minded consideration to the statutory criteria without having had specific knowledge of the section 149 obligation – they will simply have demonstrated the matters set out above. But it is to be hoped that this sort of dispute will be increasingly rare. Given the proliferation of authorities on the PSED in possession cases, social housing providers would now be well-advised to train their staff properly, or at least provide *pro forma* impact assessments that guide decision-makers clearly and accurately.

Inquiries & evidence-gathering

As noted above ('2.3 Triggering compliance' and '2.4 Evidence'), the PSED – strictly speaking – imposes a duty of inquiry on the landlord. Like other public law duties, it implies a duty of 'reasonable' inquiry[105], which requires the landlord to be properly informed before taking a decision[106].

In practice, though, the courts have recognised that: 'A duty of inquiry may well arise: it depends on the context'[107] (emphasis added), and that it can often fall to the tenant, instead, to prove their case. But landlords should be wary that the duty may fall upon them. In *Forward v Aldwyck* the breach of the PSED took the form – partly – of failing to obtain more evidence about a known disability[108]. A circuit judge has also suggested

[105] *R (Sheakh) v Lambeth LBC* [2022] PTSR 1315, [2022] EWCA Civ 457, per Sir Keith Lindblom SPT, Males & Laing LJJ at [10], citing *Secretary of State for Education & Science v Tameside MBC* [1977] AC 1014. The Court of Appeal in *Sheakh* made the point at [73] that it will only be unlawful for a public authority not to make a particular inquiry if it was irrational for it not to do so.

[106] *R (Brown) v Secretary of State for Work & Pensions* [2009] PTSR 1506, [2008] EWHC 3158 (Admin), per Scott Baker and Aikens LJJ at [85].

[107] *Forward v Aldwyck HG* [2019] HLR 20, [2019] HLR 24 (QB), per Cheema-Grubb J at [40].

[108] [2020] 1 WLR 584, [2019] EWCA Civ 1334, per Longmore LJ at [12].

that the PSED may involve obtaining specialist expertise about a disability in a particularly difficult situation[109].

Retrospective compliance

The reported cases show that there are often times where landlords have been in breach of the PSED at a certain point in the proceedings, and have then retrospectively sought to 'cure' the breach by complying late.

Both the High Court and the Court of Appeal have made it clear that it is notionally possible to comply late[110]. While it is important to scrutinise attempts at retrospective compliance (given the risk of confirmation bias), it is permissible as long as the breach no longer has any continuing significance[111]. It will therefore be important to ask, for example, what the effects of the proceedings have been. Have they particularly affected a disabled person or exacerbated their mental ill-health? Has the defendant had to prove points that the landlord should have investigated itself, such as abuse from neighbours? Has the defendant had their disability doubted or belittled?

'Then & now' challenges

Because it is an ongoing duty, the PSED can sometimes create what Fordham J has called 'then and now' challenges[112]. In other words, as the litigation has continued, the way in which the public authority is alleged to have breached the PSED might have changed. At the time of the final hearing, the court may be concerned either with a 'then' challenge

---

[109] *Rosebery HA v Williams* (unrep.) [2021] 12 WLUK 464, per HHJ Luba KC at [151].

[110] *Taylor v Slough BC* [2021] HLR 28, [2020] EWHC 3520 (Ch), per Zacaroli J at [41-42], endorsed in *TM v Metropolitan HT* [2022] 1 WLR 2161, [2021] EWCA Civ 1890, per Nugee LJ at [47].

[111] *TM v Metropolitan HT* [2022] 1 WLR 2161, [2021] EWCA Civ 1890, per Nugee LJ at [48].

[112] *R (Rowley) v Minister for the Cabinet Office* [2022] 1 WLR 1189, [2021] EWHC 2108 (Admin), at [10].

(concerning the landlord's initial decision to evict), or a 'now' challenge (concerning the ongoing breach at the time of trial), or both.

2.6 Defending the claim

While there is no strict requirement to file a defence in advance of the first possession hearing[113], it is generally advisable to prepare at least a draft defence. It may be particularly important to do so in PSED cases: partly because the defence may act as a 'trigger' by alerting the landlord to any equality issues (see 2.3 Triggering compliance, above); partly to explain to the court how any why any already-prepared impact assessment is inadequate; and partly to explain the tenant's case as to why any breach is important (see '2.10 Consequences of breach', below).

For PSED purposes, the role of the defence is to set out the nature and extent of the protected characteristic, how the PSED has been breached, and why it matters on the particular facts of the case. Given the 'then and now' nature of PSED challenges, it may be helpful for the drafter to preserve their client's position on any future breaches that might take place up to (or even during) the trial.

Tenants' representatives might be concerned about giving too much away: they may be worried that there is a risk that the landlord, armed with a defence specifying exactly what the PSED requires, might simply go away and comply as requested, robbing the tenant of a defence. All of this, of course, is fact-specific and a matter of professional judgment. But in general, lawyers may wish to resist the temptation to draft elusive or incomprehensible defences. Not only is a sensible landlord likely to re-comply with this continuing duty at some point during the proceedings anyway (particularly after the Court of Appeal's clear expression of frustration about the lack of administrative review in *TM v Metropolitan*), but any retrospective compliance is likely to bring the issue of

[113] CPR 55.7(2) specifically excuses the defendant from filing a defence in possession proceedings, and entitles them to take part in the hearing regardless – although there may be costs consequences.

confirmation bias into play. And judges, as a rule, tend to prefer clear and precise statements of case.

Unless the social landlord is entitled to (and chooses to) use the 'accelerated procedure' for ending assured shorthold tenancies under section 21 of the Housing Act 1988[114], the claim will be listed for an early possession hearing, the date of which will be notified to the parties when the court issues the claim form[115]. At that hearing, the court will decide whether the claim is 'genuinely disputed on grounds that appear to be substantial'. In a defended claim this has the same meaning as the test for summary judgment (whether the defence has a realistic prospect of success); in an undefended claim the court is concerned with whether the tenant ought to be given the opportunity to plead a defence[116].

There is useful judicial guidance on the correct approach to 'realistic prospect of success'[117], some of which is of obvious relevance in PSED challenges. 'Realistic' means more than merely 'fanciful' or 'arguable'. The court must not conduct a mini-trial, so it may be inappropriate to consider difficult issues such as whether there has been 'due' regard in the specific context of the case, or whether a condition amounts to a disability. The court may take into account the evidence that can reasonably be expected to be available at trial, even if it is not before the court yet (this is particularly helpful if there is a dispute about whether or to what extent the tenant is disabled).

Aside from the general 'reasonable prospects of success' test, the PSED is often pleaded alongside substantive discrimination cases, and it may be possible to 'piggy-back' on the more specialised test applicable to those:

---

114 Or its new equivalent under section 173 of the Renting Homes (Wales) Act 2016.

115 CPR 55.5(1).

116 CPR 55.8(2), *Global 100 v Laleva* [2022] 1 WLR 1046, [2021] EWCA Civ 135.

117 *Easyair Ltd v Opal Telecom Ltd* (unrep.) [2009] EWHC 339 (Ch), per Lewison J at [15].

the Supreme Court has said that it would not normally be appropriate to determine discrimination matters summarily, because there are often disputed facts or assessment that require disclosure or expert evidence might be required[118]. And that logic, in some cases, might also apply to PSED disputes in their own right.

There will, on the other hand, be cases where it is perfectly appropriate for the court to grasp the nettle and decide a weak PSED defence summarily.

2.7 Pre-trial practicalities

Given that the PSED is a continuing duty, landlords are under a fairly unusual statutory obligation to actively reconsider their position throughout the litigation process. In some cases there will be obvious 'triggers' for re-compliance with the PSED (such as medical evidence becoming available[119]). But in virtually every case, the landlord will know more by the time of the trial than it did when it initially decided to claim possession. There will have been statements of case, disclosure, witness evidence, and a continually-evolving set of facts (whether, for example, the tenant's conduct or health has got better or worse, or whether the defendant has been proved right that the landlord had unfairly blamed the tenant and overlooked the conduct of neigbours). Knowing the luck of social housing practitioners, there may even have been one or two new authorities since the claim was issued.

In virtually every case, therefore, landlords would be well-advised to re-comply with the PSED shortly before the trial: close enough to the trial date that they can take the latest possible information into account; distant enough that the tenant is not unfairly prejudiced by the landlord

118 *Aster Communities v Akerman-Livingstone* [2015] AC 1300, [2015] UKSC 15, per Lord Neuberger PSC at [60].

119 *TM v Metropolitan HT* [2022] 1 WLR 2161, [2021] EWCA Civ 1890; *Patrick v London & Quadrant HT* [2020] HLR 3, [2019] EWHC 1263 (QB), per Turner J at [21].

relying on very-late evidence. From the tenant's perspective, such new evidence will need to be scrutinised for self-serving assessments, or backwards reasoning that merely justifies the decision to evict, or for assessments that fail to take more recent developments seriously (see '2.5 Aspects of compliance; avoiding confirmation bias', above).

As Green LJ said in *TM v Metropolitan*, some cases cry out for administrative review[120]. A conscientious PSED assessment in that case, and a consequential change-of-mind, would have saved the costs of a week-long multi-track trial and two appeals, not to mention the impact on the tenant and his family. HHJ Luba KC made a similar point in the *Rosebery* case[121]. In serious disability cases, genuine open-minded compliance during the course of proceedings is not only essential from the perspective of complying with the law, but as a matter of practicality and cost the PSED should cause landlords to reflect seriously on whether the claim should be continued.

Disclosure is particularly interesting in PSED cases. The tenant is often making an argument about the impact of an eviction and/or structural disadvantage, and the landlord will tend to be in a much better position to provide that sort of information than the tenant. If the tenant is arguing, for example, that the use of 'absolute and mandatory' grounds for possession will have a disproportionate impact on people with psychiatric disabilities, it would be useful to ask the landlord whether it collects any data on the number of disabled tenants whom it has sought to evict, and – if not – why not. The PSED itself can require public authorities to monitor and release data concerning the impact of their decisions[122], and tenants' representatives may wish to put this aspect of the PSED to good use.

---

120 [2022] 1 WLR 2161, [2021] EWCA Civ 1890, per Green LJ at [67].

121 *Rosebery HA v Williams* (unrep.) [2021] 12 WLUK 464, per HHJ Luba KC at [151].

122 See, e.g. *R (Unison) v Lord Chancellor* [2016] 1 CMLR 25, [2015] EWCA Civ 935, per Underhill LJ at [121]: the PSED at least requires 'a reasonable and rational view about what effects a particular policy is likely to have'. The

As another example, if (as in the *Guinness v England* case[123]) the tenant is complaining that there has been racist bullying by other tenants, the PSED may require the landlord to turn its mind to the racial diversity of its tenants and the nature of its recorded complaints. If a landlord has a rent arrears policy that is bound to affect benefits-capped tenants disproportionately, that is likely to have a particular impact on women[124]. In appropriate cases, tenants' representatives may wish to use the PSED as a tool for obliging landlords to record and disclose the equality aspects of their practices and decisions.

2.8 Questioning the decision-maker

One of the rare things about running a PSED defences in possession proceedings is that it is a public law challenge where the decision-maker tends to be called as a live witness and cross-examined. There are plenty of examples of public law judges scrutinising written PSED assessments and either accepting them or rejecting them, but it is unusual for a litigant to be able to put documents to a decision-maker, and to take them to task personally on their compliance with the law.

Again, however, judicial appetites for the fruits of cross-examination are fact-specific. In *Powell v Dacorum* the district judge, the circuit judge and the Court of Appeal were all fairly unimpressed with the 'testing' exercise that was carried out in questioning, even though the witness accepted that she had not heard of some of the aspects the PSED[125], and the tenant's appeal was dismissed. But in *TM v Metropolitan* the witness had

failure to collect such impact evidence may be challenged, but only on a *Wednesbury* basis: see e.g. *R (Khalsa Academies Trust) v Secretary of State for Education* (unrep.) [2021] EWHC 2660, per Mr Gavin Mansfield QC at [111(ii)].

123 *Legal Action*, October 2019.

124 *R (SG) v Secretary of State for Work & Pensions* [2015] 1 WLR 1449, [2015] UKSC 16, per Lord Reed at [2].

125 [2019] HLR 21, [2019] EWCA Civ 23, per McCombe LJ at [34, 38].

conceded that his breach of the PSED probably would have made a difference, and – while the trial judge and the High Court granted no remedy to the tenant – the Court of Appeal dismissed the claim[126]. Both *Forward v Aldwyck* and *Luton CHT v Durdana* fall somewhere in the middle: the courts were critical of the witness's approach to the PSED and found that they had breached the duty, but nonetheless found that proper compliance would have made no difference[127].

What unites all of those cases, though, is that the quality of the evidence leaps from the pages of the judgment. Whether there has been professionalism, compassion and open-mindedness, or whether there has been recusancy, poor training and single-mindedness, the questioning of the witnesses took the cases well beyond what was written in the impact assessments themselves.

It is important to note that the Court of Appeal strongly suggested, in *TM v Metropolitan*, that it would be very difficult indeed for a decision-maker to comply with the PSED in the course of giving live evidence. They recognised that they could not be too prescriptive about this, and that there might be cases where 'some minor point [...] had been overlooked', but the thrust of the judgment is that compliance in the witness box would generally be very difficult indeed[128].

126 [2022] 1 WLR 2161, [2021] EWCA Civ 1890.

127 [2020] 1 WLR 584, [2019] EWCA Civ 1334; [2020] HLR 19, [2020] EWCA Civ 445.

128 [2022] 1 WLR 2161, [2021] EWCA Civ 1890, per Nugee LJ at [39, 47] and Green LJ at [65-66].

2.9 Consequences of a breach

Where a breach of the PSED has been established, it does not automatically follow that the claim for possession will be dismissed.

It is now well-settled that section 31(2A) of the Senior Courts Act 1981 applies to PSED defences in the County Court[129]. That section is technically a statutory test for granting a remedy in judicial review proceedings: it prohibits the Administrative Court from granting a remedy if it is 'highly likely' that the outcome would have been the same if the contravention had not occurred. In other words: if the court thinks that it is highly likely that compliance with the PSED would have made no difference, the court cannot grant a remedy (the appropriate remedy, in most cases, being the dismissal of the claim). This is the approach that County Court judges must now adopt.

If, on the other hand, the court concludes that the 'highly likely' test is not satisfied, it may grant a remedy, but remedy in public law proceedings is always a discretionary matter[130].

When applying the 'highly likely' test, it is important to emphasise that the courts should not substitute their own view as to whether compliance with the PSED would or should have made a difference. Instead, the correct approach is for the judge to determine whether the landlord would have done anything differently if the breach had not occurred[131].

Again, it is difficult to predict how judges will approach individual cases, except by looking at the small class of outliers that make up the reported decisions. In both *Forward v Aldwyck* and *Luton CHT v Durdana*, the breach of the PSED was of little relevance to the claim: in *Forward* the

---

129 *Forward v Aldwyck HG* [2020] 1 WLR 584, [2019] EWCA Civ 1334, per Longmore LJ at [36].

130 See e.g. *R (Elkundi) v Birmingham CC* [2022] QB 604, [2022] EWCA Civ 601, per Lewis LJ at [129].

131 *Luton CHT v Durdana* [2020] HLR 19, [2020] EWCA Civ 445, per Patten LJ at [33].

tenant had a physical disability with little bearing on his factual assertion that he was being targeted by drug dealers as a result of an unproved mental health condition; in *Durdana* there were relatively serious disabilities in the household, but they were not very closely connected with the ground for possession (obtaining the tenancy by false statements)[132]. In *TM*, on the other hand, the Court of Appeal was particularly concerned that Metropolitan had prosecuted the claim against a defendant who lacked capacity to participate in the proceedings: 'He therefore suffered direct prejudice from the failure properly to perform the PSED which would (or should) have revealed his incapacity and the prejudice he faced in being subjected to possession proceedings'[133]. In two other first instance cases, the breach of the PSED formed part of a catalogue of errors and omissions by the landlords[134]. Landlords will be keen to cite Longmore LJ's point that the courts should not 'act as some sort of mentor or nanny to decision-makers'[135], while tenants will cite the powerful and sympathetic reasoning of Nugee and Green LJJ in *TM v Metropolitan.*

2.10 The enforcement stage

In the early PSED cases, judicial thinking reflected the idea that a landlord who was in breach of the PSED when a possession order was made could simply do it later, for example at the warrant stage. More recent decisions, though, seem to lean against that principle.

---

132 [2020] 1 WLR 584, [2019] EWCA Civ 1334; [2020] HLR 19, [2020] EWCA Civ 445.

133 [2022] 1 WLR 2161, [2021] EWCA Civ 1890, per Nugee LJ at [64].

134 *Guinness Partnership v England* (*Legal Action*, October 2019); *Rosebery HA v Williams* (unrep.) [2021] 12 WLUK 464.

135 *Forward v Aldwyck HG* [2020] 1 WLR 584, [2019] EWCA Civ 1334, at [25].

In the first PSED possession case, *Barnsley v Norton*[136], the Court of Appeal said that the landlord could comply with the PSED post-eviction, and could even do so while it was determining the family's homelessness application, even though such compliance would involve completely different considerations. This idea was picked up more recently in *Durdana*, where the landlord argued that it could comply with the PSED when deciding whether to apply for a warrant. The trial judge had rejected this because of the 'risk that [the landlord], armed with a possession order, would not approach the evaluation exercise required with an open mind'[137], and the Court of Appeal also changed course from its decision in *Norton*. Rather than relying on the idea that the landlord could defer compliance, the more up-to-date approach seems to be that the court should instead focus on whether any breach established at trial is or was material, and decide whether or not to dismiss the claim on that basis[138].

This idea was bolstered in *TM v Metropolitan*, in which the Court of Appeal emphasised the risk of 'confirmation bias' and endorsed the idea that retrospective compliance is only permissible where the initial breach no longer has any continuing significance[139]. But it is difficult to assess whether future, notional compliance at the enforcement stage might meet these conditions. In practice, therefore, at the trial stage, the courts are likely to focus on the question of the materiality of any existing or prior breach in deciding whether or not to make a possession order, rather than overlooking breaches and allowing landlords to defer compliance to a later date.

136 [2012] PTSR 54, [2011] EWCA Civ 834, per Lloyd LJ at [22]. Cited with approval in *Powell v Dacorum MBC* [2019] HLR 21, [2019] EWCA Civ 23, per McCombe LJ at [42].

137 [2020] HLR 19, [2020] EWCA Civ 445, per Patten LJ at [25], citing HHJ Bloom.

138 Ibid. at [28-36]

139 [2022] 1 WLR 2161, [2021] EWCA Civ 1890, per Nugee LJ at [48].

That is not to say that warrant stage disputes will not arise. There may be cases in which circumstances have changed, new evidence has become available, or the PSED was not cited earlier. In some cases, it will be appropriate to raise a PSED point attacking the landlord's decision to apply for enforcement of the possession order. But the High Court has made it clear that landlords are not necessarily bound to explicitly re-comply at the warrant stage if there has been no change in circumstances[140].

As to the procedure for citing the PSED at the warrant stage, it is probably possible to bring a claim for judicial review, but it seems more convenient to litigate the point in the possession proceedings instead. That was the approach taken in *Powell v Dacorum* (no criticism was made by the Court of Appeal)[141], and the courts have pointed out that it can be more pragmatic to raise public law points in possession proceedings[142].

2.11 Where next?

All of the reported PSED possession cases concern the protected characteristic of disability. But it will be interesting to see whether race begins to play a more prominent role in this area of law, given the growing awareness of structural racism in the social housing sector.

The first instance cases have perhaps already begun to sow the seeds of this. In *Guinness v England* the landlord had failed to take the tenant's complaints about racist bullying seriously, and this position unravelled in the course of the proceedings when video evidence was produced[143]. In a 2020 case concerning negligent misstatement, a housing association

---

140 *Patrick v London & Quadrant HT* [2020] HLR 3, [2019] EWHC 1263 (QB), per Turner J at [42(v)].

141 [2019] HLR 21, [2019] EWCA Civ 23.

142 *Arkin v Marshall (HLPA intervening)* [2020] 1 WLR 3284, [2020] EWCA Civ 620, per Sir Geoffrey Vos C at [15].

143 *Legal Action*, October 2019.

was ordered to pay more than £30,000 in damages when it failed to tell a Black tenant during a mutual exchange process that a neighbouring tenant had a history of carrying out racist abuse against the former occupier[144]. In disrepair cases, leading housing law specialist Giles Peaker has said that it is common for social landlords to make accusations of 'ritual bathing' in damp and mould cases brought by African households[145].

It is precisely this sort of issue that the PSED is designed to highlight and eliminate. Harassment – which is specifically targeted by the PSED – involves 'creating an intimidating, hostile, degrading, humiliating or offensive environment'[146], and possession proceedings may be the forum in which these sorts of issues finally become exposed. While some might see this sort of PSED challenge as something of an overreach, others might take the view that it is entirely appropriate that a provision designed to root out structural racism after the death of Stephen Lawrence should be used as a tool of anti-racism in the social housing sector.

It may also be possible to use the PSED as the basis for challenging an underlying policy, such as a possession or anti-social behaviour policy. The process of reasoning is slightly tenuous, but theoretically sound:

- It is unlawful to formulate a policy in breach of the PSED[147];

---

[144] *TJ v London &t Quadrant Housing Trust* (unrep.), see Giles Peaker, 'The things you never told me…', *Nearly Legal: Housing Law News and Comment* (www.nearlylegal.co.uk).

[145] Giles Peaker, 'An Avoidable Death', *Nearly Legal: Housing Law News and Comment* (www.nearlylegal.co.uk).

[146] Equality Act 2010, section 26.

[147] See, e.g. *R (Ward & Gullu) v Hillingdon LBC* [2019] PTSR 1738, [2019] EWCA Civ 692.

- Decisions made pursuant to unlawful policies (including a decision to evict) are, themselves, also unlawful[148];

- The courts – including the County Court in a possession claim – cannot give effect to an unlawful act[149]; and

- While a policy challenge is normally brought by judicial review, the courts have recognised that 'considerations of justice and pragmatism' may make it appropriate for public law challenges to be brought in private law proceedings[150].

Does the landlord's policy on the use of 'absolute and mandatory grounds' have a disproportionate impact on tenants with behavioural disabilities? Will a rent arrears policy have the effect of displacing single parents – more likely to be women – out of the local area? Does a discretionary second succession policy of a landlord with a particularly high number of Bangladeshi tenants adequately take into account kinship ties and obligations? These are anxious questions. As long as there remain extraordinarily wide gaps in housing outcomes with regard to most – if not all – of the protected characteristics, we are bound to see PSED challenges in the courts.

---

148 *Alibkheit v Brent LBC* [2019] HLR 15, [2018] EWCA Civ 2742, per Lewison LJ at [47-49].

149 *Lewisham LBC v Malcolm* [2008] 1 AC 1399, [2008] UKHL 43, per Lord Bingham at [7]. Before it was put on a statutory footing under section 35 of the Equality Act 2010, this was the basis on which tenants were entitled to plead discrimination as a defence to possession proceedings.

150 *Arkin v Marshall (HLPA intervening)* [2020] 1 WLR 3284, [2020] EWCA Civ 620, per Sir Geoffrey Vos C at [15].

CHAPTER THREE

HOMELESSNESS

3.1 A viable ground of appeal

The Court of Appeal established that the PSED is a legitimate ground of appeal in homelessness challenges shortly before the current duty came into force[151]. In *Pieretti v Enfield LBC* the local authority had argued that the PSED only applied to the 'macro' functions of public authorities – for example formulating policies – but the Court of Appeal held that it also applies to functions that concerned 'micro' or individualised decision-making. This included homelessness review decisions under sections 202-203 of the Housing Act 1996[152].

Indeed, the Supreme Court has explicitly said that the PSED can succeed as a complete and free-standing ground of appeal. In the leading case, *Hotak v Southwark*, Lord Neuberger said at [79] that: 'there will undoubtedly be cases where a review, which was otherwise lawful, will be held unlawful because it does not comply with the equality duty'[153].

The Court of Appeal has more recently shown some signs of doubt about whether the PSED, alone, could defeat an otherwise-lawful review decision. In *McMahon v Watford BC*, Lewison LJ pointed out that neither Lord Neuberger nor counsel who had appeared in *McMahon* could identify any compelling examples (except for procedural points) of a decision that assessed the applicant's case in compliance with the substantive homelessness legislation, but which had nevertheless

---

151 *Pieretti v Enfield LBC* [2011] PTSR 565, [2010] EWCA Civ 1104.

152 Ibid. per Wilson LJ at [26].

153 [2016] AC 811, [2015] UKSC 30. Strictly speaking this point arose in *Kanu v Southwark LBC*, one of the two cases heard jointly with *Hotak*.

breached the PSED[154]. The Court of Appeal warned against applicants using the PSED as a technical pretext for attacking 'otherwise unimpeachable' decisions[155]. But Lewison LJ's doubts about the possibility of the PSED as a standalone ground are probably limited to the issue of vulnerability: in two other cases, concerning the adequacy of the applicant's accommodation, Lewison LJ himself quashed the review decisions on the sole basis of a breach of the PSED[156].

As in other contexts, the purpose of the PSED is not to achieve a particular result. The PSED is a process duty, and a PSED challenge is an attack upon the way in which the decision was reached[157]. But this does not diminish the importance of the duty[158].

In essence, the PSED is a mandatory consideration: section 149 is something that decision makers must take into account, where relevant, in reaching decisions on the applicant's homelessness rights. Its purpose, in the homelessness context, has been described by the Court of Appeal as being: 'to bring equality issues into the mainstream, so that they become an essential element in public decision-making'; considerations of equality of opportunity (where they arise) are to be 'placed at the centre of formulation' of homelessness decisions[159]. Compliance with the PSED – whether it is demonstrated by explicit words or not – will allow the

---

154 [2020] PTSR 1217, [2020] EWCA Civ 497, at [51].

155 Ibid. at [89].

156 *Lomax v Gosport BC* [2019] PTSR 167, [2018] EWCA Civ 1846; *Kannan v Newham LBC* [2019] HLR 22, [2019] EWCA Civ 57.

157 *Hotak v Southwark LBC* [2016] AC 811, [2015] UKSC 30, per Lord Neuberger at [73].

158 *R (Bridges) v Chief Constable of South Wales Police* [2020] 1 WLR 5064, [2020] EWCA Civ 1058, per Sir Terence Etherton MR, Dame Victoria Sharp PQBD & Singh LJ at [176].

159 *Haque v Hackney LBC* [2017] PTSR 769, [2017] EWCA Civ 4, per Briggs LJ at [21].

decision-maker to determine the applicant's statutory rights with a full awareness of the equality implications of the case.

The Court of Appeal has accepted a characterisation of the duty as being: 'the task of the reviewing officer is not to label; it is to understand'[160]. In other words the PSED is not a cosmetic exercise, and compliance (or breach) will be determined by the substance of the decision, and not by any particular wording. Equally, though, equality issues can only be understood if it the PSED has been performed 'in substance, with rigour, and with an open mind'[161]. Both of those are powerful, attractive statements of the law, and this is the nub of PSED disputes: some judges (and local authority lawyers) will see the facts of a given case and reach for the authorities decrying 'nit-picking' and 'over-zealous' critiques of language; others (and applicants' lawyers) will emphasise the disadvantages faced by people with disabilities, and highlight the need for conscientious, frank decision-making.

While some protected characteristics will be more or less relevant than others in a given situation, there is no formal 'hierarchy' of protected characteristics that promotes the importance of one over the others[162].

Although the PSED (in general) is a personal and non-delegable duty, where the local authority has contracted-out its homelessness decision making, the contractor is entitled to perform the duty on behalf of the council: anything done by the contractor is to be treated as having been done by the local authority itself[163].

---

160 *McMahon v Watford BC* [2020] PTSR 1217, [2020] EWCA Civ 497, per Lewison LJ at [68].

161 *Hotak v Southwark LBC* [2016] AC 811, [2015] UKSC 30, per Lord Neuberger at [78].

162 *Biden v Waverley BC* [2022] PTSR 1056, [2022] EWCA Civ 442, per Macur LJ at [54-56].

163 *Panayioutou v Waltham Forest* (more accurately, *Smith v Haringey*) [2018] QB 1232, [2017] EWCA Civ 1624, per Lewison LJ at [79].

3.2 Triggering compliance

In summary, and assuming that it is relevant, local authorities will be required to comply with the PSED:

- Where the need to comply is obvious;
- Where the applicant invites them to consider the PSED; and/or
- Where the evidence raises a 'real possibility' that there may be a relevant equality issue.

The PSED only arises where the applicant is under a protected characteristic which is in some way relevant to any particular aspect(s) of homelessness rights that the local authority is required to determine in a given case[164]. In other words, the PSED does not arise in every case, but only where some equality aspect is relevant. Even though every applicant will have a number of protected characteristics, and every application will require a number of issues to be determined, the PSED can often be safely ignored. For example, if an applicant is seriously disabled but their migration status renders them ineligible for assistance, there can be no realistic argument that the local authority must focus sharply on disability when reaching an eligibility decision.

The Court of Appeal has been clear that compliance is triggered not only where it has been <u>established</u> that the applicant has a protected characteristic, but also where some feature of the evidence presents a 'real possibility' that the applicant has a relevant protected characteristic[165].

The Court of Appeal has been equally clear that applicants themselves do not need to explicitly raise disability. In *Pieretti* Wilson LJ said that the

---

[164] *Pieretti v Enfield LBC* [2011] PTSR 565, [2010] EWCA Civ 1104, per Wilson LJ at [35-36], applied in *Hotak v Southwark LBC* [2016] AC 811, [2015] UKSC 30, per Lord Neuberger at [77].

[165] *Pieretti v Enfield LBC* [2011] PTSR 565, [2010] EWCA Civ 1104, per Wilson LJ at [35].

PSED is designed to foster a culture of greater awareness of disability-related issues, 'including the fact that a disabled person may not be adept at proclaiming his disability'[166]. This principle modified the earlier judicial thinking that homelessness appeals should generally be constrained to issues that were either obvious, or had been specifically raised by the applicant. This, of course, does not preclude an applicant or their advisers from raising disability or the PSED in representations as a way of triggering or ensuring compliance, and applicants would often be well-advised to be as clear and explicit about the PSED as possible, even where the evidence had passed that 'real possibility' test.

It is worth noting that the threshold for 'disability' is low. Section 6 of the Equality Act 2010, read with section 212, has the effect that a person is under the protected characteristic of disability if they have a physical or mental impairment which has an adverse effect on their ability to carry out normal day-to-day activities, and the effect is more than minor or trivial. Thus the PSED has a very light trigger: an applicant must merely present a 'real possibility' of a condition that has a 'more than minimal' effect on their daily living, assuming that the disability is in some way relevant.

There are three medical conditions that always constitute disabilities, regardless of severity: cancer, multiple sclerosis and HIV[167]. There are also a number of conditions which regulations exclude from the definition of disability. These include substance addiction, tendency to start fires, tendency to steal, tendency to commit physical or sexual abuse, exhibitionism and voyeurism[168]. There is also statutory guidance on the definition of disability, which contains some useful practical examples and case studies[169]. This guidance is particularly useful where there is an

[166] Ibid. at [28].

[167] Equality Act 2010, schedule 1 para 6.

[168] Equality Act 2010 (Disability) Regulations 2010, regs. 3-4.

[169] 'Equality Act 2010 Guidance: Guidance on matters to be taken into account in determining questions relating to the definition of disability', Office for Disability Issues.

overlap between excluded conditions and other disabilities, for example where mental ill-health gives rise to substance misuse. Courts must take that guidance into account where it is relevant[170].

If it is unclear whether the PSED applies, or whether it is relevant, the duty itself may oblige reviewing officers to carry out further inquiries to reach an answer, so that they make their decision from a properly-informed perspective[171] (see '3.3 Inquiries', below).

Presumably, where it has been established that an applicant's condition does not meet the definition of disability, the PSED (insofar as it is relevant to disability) falls away[172]. But local authorities should resist the temptation to reach a conclusion that an applicant is not disabled, simply with a view to avoiding compliance with the duty. This approach may simply give rise to other grounds of appeal. While it is, ostensibly, impermissible for an applicant to raise a direct factual challenge to the question of whether they are disabled[173], the local authority may find itself vulnerable to grounds of appeal asserting irrationality, failure to take account of relevant matters, mishandling the medical evidence[174], or misdirection in law as to the low threshold for establishing disability.

---

170 Equality Act 2010, schedule 1 para 12. The guidance is issued pursuant to sub-section 6(5) of the Act.

171 *R (Hurley & Moore) v Secretary of State for Business, Education & Skills* [2012] HRLR 13, [2012] EWHC 201 (Admin) per Elias LJ at [89-90], cited in the homelessness context in *Hotak v Southwark LBC* [2016] AC 811, [2015] UKSC 30, per Lord Neuberger at [77] (cf. *TM v Metropolitan HT* [2022] 1 WLR 2161, [2021] EWCA Civ 1890, per Nugee LJ at [44]: *Hurley & Moore* was not a contentious issue in *Hotak*, and Lord Nueberger had not heard argument on whether it is correct).

172 See e.g. *Swan HA v Gill* [2014] HLR 18, [2013] EWCA Civ 1556, a possession case.

173 *Adesotu v Lewisham LBC* [2019] 1 WLR 5636, [2019] EWCA Civ 1405, per Bean LJ at [18].

174 See, e.g., *Guiste v Lambeth LBC* [2020] HLR 12, [2020] EWCA Civ 1758.

3.3 Inquires

In homelessness matters generally, the burden of inquiries is on the local authority and it is not for the applicant to prove their case. The local authority is generally required to carry out such inquiries as are necessary to 'satisfy' itself as to the matters necessary for establishing the applicant's rights, and it is open to an applicant to challenge that process – but only if the inquiries were deficient on a *Wednesbury* basis[175].

Where the PSED arises, though, the general principles of homelessness law must be applied slightly differently. In *Cramp v Hastings* the Court of Appeal had held that homelessness appeals should generally only concern issues if the applicant had raised them, or if they were obvious[176]. But in *Pieretti*, shortly afterwards, the Court of Appeal realised that this principle needed to be qualified when the PSED was in play: an additional or enhanced duty of inquiry applies where there is a real possibility of a relevant disability, and local authorities may need to consider disability-related points that were not explicitly raised by the applicant.[177]

This is because the PSED 'is designed to secure the brighter illumination of a person's disability so that, to the extent that it bears upon his rights under other laws, it attracts a full appraisal'[178]. In other words, in order to reach a decision from a perspective that is fully-informed as to equality rights, the PSED may require local authorities to take a more proactive approach to their inquiries in appropriate cases. This may, for example,

[175] See, e.g. *Biden v Waverley BC* [2022] PTSR 1056, [2022] EWCA Civ 442, per Macur LJ at [48].

[176] [2005] 4 All ER 1014, [2005] EWCA Civ 1014.

[177] [2011] PTSR 565, [2010] EWCA Civ 1104, per Wilson LJ at [32, 35], applied in *Birmingham CC v Wilson* [2017] HLR 4, [2016] EWCA Civ 1137, per Sales LJ at [33].

[178] *Pieretti v Enfield LBC* [2011] PTSR 565, [2010] EWCA Civ 1104, per Wilson LJ at [26].

oblige the decision-maker to seek medical expertise[179]. The English statutory code of guidance advises local authorities that the PSED requires them to 'collect sufficient information to develop a reasonable understanding of what the equality impacts might be'[180].

But this, too, has its limits. In *Biden v Waverley BC*, the applicant was a trans woman whose case was that the reviewing officer ought to have made out-of-the-ordinary inquiries regarding hate crime in the local area, relying on the 'enhanced' duty of inquiry established in *Pieretti*. The Court of Appeal dismissed as 'absurd' the suggestion that it was unlawful for the local authority to have failed to expand the scope of its inquiries to include the opinions of an LGBT liaison officer. On the facts of that particular case the authority's inquiries were not deficient on a *Wednesbury* basis, and the reviewing officer's overall approach demonstrated that she had complied with the PSED[181].

3.4 Aspects of compliance

In practical terms, asserting a breach of the PSED has a great deal in common with other aspects of homelessness law[182]:

- The reviewing officer is under a duty to give reasons as to the PSED, but that duty is no different from the general statutory duty under section 203(4) of the Housing Act 1996;

---

179 See, e.g. *Shala v Birmingham CC* [2008] HLR 8, [2007] EWCA Civ 624. While *Shala* is not a PSED decision, the Court of Appeal appears to have impliedly acknowledged that its central point has some bearing in PSED cases: *Biden v Waverley BC* [2022] PTSR 1056, [2022] EWCA Civ 442, per Macur LJ at [52].

180 Homelessness code of guidance for local authorities, §1.15(b).

181 [2022] PTSR 1056, [2022] EWCA Civ 442, per Macur LJ at [53, 60].

182 *McMahon v Watford BC* [2020] PTSR 1217, [2020] EWCA Civ 497, per Lewison LJ at [14-18].

- It is for the applicant to show that the reviewing officer has breached the PSED, and not for the local authority to show that they have not; and

- The courts should adopt a benevolent approach to decisions, rather than a technical or 'nit-picking' one.

As with every context in which it arises, the courts' approach to assessing compliance with the PSED in homelessness matters is highly case-specific. In *Hotak*, the Supreme Court recognised that it was not possible to be particularly 'precise or prescriptive' about compliance with the PSED, even when giving judgment in a leading case[183]. Similarly, in *Haque* the Court of Appeal warned the courts to be 'appropriately cautious when invited to treat any part of the judgment in a leading case as if it were of statutory force, with a general effect dissociated from the particular facts under review'[184]. It is difficult even to cite the homelessness authorities without cautioning the court that each case was explicitly decided on a particularly fact-specific basis.

And there is not even uniform judicial thinking regarding the same set of facts: in *Haque* McCombe LJ gave a short additional judgment confessing to 'having had hesitation' at concluding that the reviewing officer had adequately demonstrated compliance with certain aspects of the PSED, but ultimately leaned against taking too nit-picking, micro-managing an approach[185].

What is clear from the authorities, though, is that PSED disputes will be particularly common in cases concerning assessments of 'vulnerability' for the purposes of section 189 if the Housing Act 1996, 'intentionality' for the purposes of section 191, and the adequacy of accommodation for the purposes of sections 175 and 193/206. This was a prediction that the

---

183 [2016] AC 811, [2015] UKSC 30, per Lord Neuberger at [74].

184 [2017] PTSR 769, [2017] EWCA Civ 4, per Briggs LJ at [41].

185 Ibid. per McComble LJ at [61-63].

Court of Appeal made in *Pieretti*[186], and has been borne out by the reported cases.

Complementary or independent?

Across the areas of homelessness dispute in which it has been argued, the PSED has been treated as a 'complementary' duty to a greater or lesser extent. The closer the overlap between the PSED and the particularly statutory question, the less that the PSED may add to the reviewing officer's duties. In *Hotak*, for example, the Supreme Court said that the PSED 'can fairly be described as complementary' to the question of vulnerability[187]. But in intentionality disputes, there is likely to a greater difference between complying with the PSED and deciding whether the applicant has 'become homeless intentionally'. Commenting on the facts of *Pieretti*, the Court of Appeal in *Haque* noted that *Pieretti* had not been 'a case in which there was any inherently close alignment between the PSED and the particular aspect of the housing duty in issue'[188].

The greater the overlap between the underlying point of homelessness and the PSED, the more likely it is that the reviewing officer will have complied with the PSED by merely performing their Housing Act obligations[189]. This is likely to lead to disputes about whether the applicant's circumstances have led to a *Hotak*-type situation – a case of close alignment – or a *Pieretti*-type situation, where there is a need for proper and separate compliance[190].

---

186 [2011] PTSR 565, [2010] EWCA Civ 1104, per Wilson LJ at [31]

187 [2016] AC 811, [2015] UKSC 30, per Lord Neuberger at [78].

188 [2017] PTSR 769, [2017] EWCA Civ 4, per Briggs LJ at [41]. See also non-homelessness cases, e.g. *McDonagh v Kensington & Chelsea* RLBC [2011] PTSR. 1266, discussed in *Haque* at [33].

189 *McMahon v Watford BC* [2020] PTSR 1217, [2020] EWCA Civ 497, per Lewison LJ at [67].

190 This dispute came up, for example, in *Hackney LBC v Haque* [2017] PTSR 769, [2017] EWCA Civ 4, per Briggs LJ at [40].

Vulnerability

The fact that an applicant satisfies the Equality Act definition of disability does not automatically mean that they are 'vulnerable' for the purposes of section 189(1)(c) of the Housing Act 1996. Disability does not confer automatic priority need for accommodation[191]. Instead, vulnerability has its own separate test: whether, when compared with an ordinary person if made homeless, the applicant, in consequence of a characteristic within section 189(1)(c), would suffer or be at risk of suffering harm or detriment which the ordinary person would not suffer or be at risk of suffering such that the harm or detriment would make a noticeable difference to his ability to deal with the consequences of homelessness[192].

The purpose of the PSED is to highlight the consequences of the applicant's disability, so that the reviewing officer can decide whether the applicant meets that 'vulnerability' test with those consequences well in mind.

The key passage for understanding compliance with the PSED in vulnerability cases is in Lord Neuberger's judgment in *Hotak* at [78]. He said that the PSED requires the reviewing officer to 'focus very sharply' on:

- Whether the applicant is under a disability, or any other relevant protected characteristic;
- The extent of such a disability;
- The likely effect of the disability, when taken together with any other features, on the applicant if and when homeless; and
- Whether the applicant is, as a result, 'vulnerable'.

---

191 *McMahon v Watford BC* [2020] PTSR 1217, [2020] EWCA Civ 497, per Lewison LJ at [73].

192 *Panayioutou v Waltham Forest* [2018] QB 1232, [2017] EWCA Civ 1624.

This four-part exercise was then considered by the Court of Appeal in two later cases: *Haque* and *McMahon v Watford BC*. In light of those two decisions:

- Local authorities are entitled to a 'fair, stand-back' reading of the decision in its context[193];
- Lord Neuberger's four matters of 'sharp focus' are not a strict or formulaic four-stage test, and reviewing officer do not need to answer each question in sequence[194];
- Lord Neuberger's four matters, ultimately, only concern the question of the applicant's ability to deal with the consequences of being homeless, and reviewing officers are therefore not required to focus sharply whether disability affects the applicant in other ways (for example their ability to carry out tasks in their workplace)[195].

The four-part *Hotak* list will, essentially, be the lens through which vulnerability decisions are read, as far as compliance with the PSED is concerned. But it will be very difficult to know what judges – tasked with applying a 'stand-back' reading – will make of each decision. In any given case, some judges might treat the PSED as a critical mechanism for shining light on disability issues, while others may deride it as a disciplinary stick for beating well-meaning reviewing officers. And, given the judicial caution about whether the PSED is even capable of operating as a standalone ground in vulnerability challenges (see '3.1 A viable ground of appeal', above), it will tend to be at its strongest precisely when it is needed least: when there is another viable ground, such as irrationality or a misreading of the medical evidence. Nevertheless,

---

[193] *Hackney LBC v Haque* [2017] PTSR 769, [2017] EWCA Civ 4, per Briggs LJ at [37, 49-51].

[194] *McMahon v Watford BC* [2020] PTSR 1217, [2020] EWCA Civ 497, per Lewison LJ at [52-53].

[195] Ibid. at [41].

homelessness applicants, their advisers, and reviewing officers should pay close attention to whether the PSED has been observed in every case.

Suitability/quality of accommodation

For suitability decisions, and decisions about whether it is reasonable for the applicant to continue to occupy their accommodation (and probably in homelessness decision-making more generally), the relevant aspect of the PSED is section 149(1)(b): the need to advance equality of opportunity[196]. This means that reviewing officers will need, in particular, to show that they have had due regard to:

- The need to remove or eliminate disadvantages suffered by protected groups;
- The need to take steps to meet the different needs of protected groups;
- The need to take account of disabilities; and
- The (potential) need to treat protected groups more favourably.

The first key passage for understanding compliance with the PSED in suitability cases is in Briggs LJ's judgment in *Haque* at [43]. On the particular facts of *Haque*, he held that that the PSED required the reviewing officer to do six things:

- Recognise that the applicant was disabled (bearing in mind the correct legal meaning of disability);
- Focus on the specific aspects of the applicant's impairments that were relevant to the suitability of his accommodation;

[196] *Hackney LBC v Haque* [2017] PTSR 769, [2017] EWCA Civ 4, per Briggs LJ at [19].

- Focus on the consequences of the applicant's impairments, achieved by comparing the disadvantages that he would suffer in his particular accommodation with any disadvantages that someone without his impairments would suffer;

- Focus on the needs that arise from the applicant's impairments (again, by comparing them to the needs of someone without his impairments), and on the extent to which the accommodation met those needs;

- Recognise that the applicant's disability-related needs might require more favourable treatment; and

- Reach a decision on suitability that paid regard to those matters.

But – again – a key point to emerge from *Haque* was that reviewing officers are entitled to a 'fair, stand-back reading' of their decisions, rather than a strict and formulaic approach to those questions[197].

Suitability challenges have a great deal in common with the question of whether accommodation is 'reasonable for the applicant to continue to occupy' their accommodation, which arises both under section 175 (whether the applicant is homeless) and section 191 (whether the applicant has become homeless intentionally). While this is a different question to suitability, for PSED purposes the exercise is very similar (if not the same). In *Lomax v Gosport BC* (a section 175 case) the Court of Appeal cited both Lord Neuberger's four-part analysis in *Hotak* and Briggs LJ's six-part analysis in *Haque*. Lewison LJ concluded by accepting a modified six-question approach[198], which might be seen as preferable to the earlier *Haque* list in cases concerning the adequacy or quality of

---

197 [2017] PTSR 769, [2017] EWCA Civ 4, per Briggs LJ at [37, 49-51].

198 *Lomax v Gosport BC* [2019] PTSR 167, [2018] EWCA Civ 1846, per Lewison LJ at [43].

accommodation (it is, with no disrespect to Briggs LJ, worded more crisply). Reviewing officers must show:

- A sharp focus on whether the applicant is disabled;
- A sharp focus on the extent of their disabilities;
- A sharp focus on the likely effect of the disabilities, when taken together with any other features, on the applicant for as long as they continued to occupy the property;
- A sharp focus on the applicant's particular needs in relation to accommodation which arise from their disabilities and the extent to which their current accommodation meets those needs;
- A comparison between the applicant's accommodation needs and the accommodation needs of people without the applicant's particular disabilities; and
- A recognition that when considering whether it was reasonable for them to continue to occupy her property the applicant might need to be treated more favourably than others without her disabilities.

Again, it is always difficult to know precisely how a particular judge is likely to approach a PSED question, but it is notable that two of the three successful PSED challenged in reported homelessness appeals – *Lomax* and *Kannan v Newham LBC*[199] – have concerned the quality of the accommodation of an applicant with a disability. There may be more scope for successful PSED challenges in this aspect of homelessness law than in vulnerability disputes.

[199] [2019] HLR 22, [2019] EWCA Civ 57. See also *HM (a protected party, by his litigation friend FM) v Southwark LBC* (*Legal Action*, December 2020/January 2021).

Intentionality

Unlike vulnerability and suitability, the question of 'becoming homeless intentionally' under section 191 of the Housing Act 1996 does not benefit from a Court of Appeal decision setting out a helpful list of guidance. The best available case is *Pieretti*, in which the Court of Appeal quashed a review decision on the basis that the local authority had failed to make adequate inquiries about a possible link between disability and intentional homelessness. There is not yet any authority that scrutinises a review decision that purports to comply with the PSED in an intentionality case[200].

It is, perhaps, unlikely that there ever will be a case that gives generic guidance in intentionality matters. Unlike vulnerability (where there is an almost-perfect overlap between the PSED and the statutory homelessness question) and suitability (where there is a fairly close overlap), intentionality is not an area where there is a particularly close relationship between the PSED and the relevant question(s). Indeed, intentionality (a complex statutory formula) gives rise to a number of different questions. It would be difficult for any court to say, authoritatively, precisely what compliance with the PSED involves in an intentionality case.

There are some situations where it is easy to envision the PSED playing a role. A tenant with a disability might have lost their home for anti-social behaviour, for example, and – because the statutory code of guidance advises that acts that can be put down to 'a temporary aberration or aberrations caused by mental illness' should not be treated as deliberate[201] – there are likely to be cases in which reviewing officers will have to focus

---

200 Except that *Lomax v Gosport BC* [2019] PTSR 167, [2018] EWCA Civ 1846 concerns section 175(3) of the Housing Act 1996, which uses the same rubric as section 191(1): 'reasonable for him to continue to occupy'. Presumably the reasoning in *Lomax* would apply in an intentionality case in which the reasonableness of the applicant's continued occupation is the issue.

201 Homelessness code of guidance for local authorities, §9.17(c).

sharply on the extent and consequences of the applicant's disabilities in assessing causation. Similarly, in affordability disputes, reviewing officers will have to pay particularly close attention to the costs of any disability-related needs, and/or the applicant's ability to manage a very tight budget. This is certainly the case in a comparable and very similar 'due regard' duty: section 11 of the Children Act 2004[202].

Otherwise, it is fairly safe to suppose that compliance with the PSED in intentionality cases would probably require:

- A sharp focus on whether the applicant is disabled, or under another relevant protected characteristic;
- A sharp focus on the extent of any disability;
- A sharp focus on the likely effects of the disability or other protected characteristic;
- A sharp focus on any disability needs; and
- An evaluation of the relevant 'intentionality' question that bears those equality issues well in mind.

'Due' regard & weight

The PSED requires 'due' regard. The courts have interpreted this as meaning the degree of regard that is 'appropriate in all the circumstances'[203]. The Supreme Court has expressed its regret that 'this was not a particularly helpful guide', but nevertheless endorsed the point, which (they said) was unavoidable because of Parliament's inclusion of

[202] *Nzolameso v Westminster CC* [2015] 2 All ER 942, [2015] UKSC 22, per Baroness Hale at [25].

[203] *Pieretti v Enfield LBC* [2011] PTSR 565, [2010] EWCA Civ 1104, per Wilson LJ at [33]. For an application in the possession context, see *Luton CHT v Durdana* [2020] HLR 19, [2020] EWCA Civ 445, per Patten LJ at [17-18].

the word 'due' in the statute. Lord Neuberger concluded: 'I do not think it is possible to be more precise or prescriptive, given that the weight and extent of the duty are highly fact-sensitive and dependent on individual judgment'[204].

What this means in practice is that the attention that reviewing officers must pay to the PSED will be different in virtually every case, depending on both the type of case and the overall relevance of the PSED to the issue in dispute. Lord Neuberger is, of course, right to say that what is 'due' is highly fact-sensitive, and it can be difficult to predict the approach that the courts may take in any given case.

This is clear from the appeal cases in which different judges have dramatically reversed outcomes even when looking at the same facts. In a high-profile challenge to the introduction to automated facial recognition software in South Wales, a Divisional Court (Haddon-Cave LJ and Swift J) said that there was an 'air of unreality' about the PSED ground and dismissed the claim. A notable constitution of the Court of Appeal (Sir Terence Etherton MR, Dame Victoria Sharp PQBD and Singh LJ) reversed them, saying: 'On the contrary, it seems to raise a serious issue of public concern'[205]. In the homelessness field, a similar thing happened in *Haque*: on the first appeal HHJ Luba QC decided that the review decision had not demonstrated compliance with the PSED even when given a 'stand back' reading; Briggs LJ held that the reviewing officer had 'plainly' complied; McCombe LJ 'had hesitation' in deciding that the reviewing officer had shown compliance; and Beatson LJ (somewhat cryptically) agreed with both Briggs and McCombe LJJ[206].

What is clear, though, is that it is for the local authority and <u>not</u> for the court to decide how much weight to give to the statutory criteria. There

---

[204] *Hotak v Southwark* [2016] AC 811, [2015] UKSC 30, *LBC*, per Lord Neuberger PSC at [74].

[205] *R (Bridges) v Chief Constable of South Wales Police* [2020] 1 WLR 5064, [2020] EWCA Civ 1058 at [173].

[206] [2017] PTSR 769, [2017] EWCA Civ 4, at [5-6, 50-51, 59, 61].

is no requirement for the PSED to be given any particular amount of weight[207]. As long as there has been 'proper and conscientious focus', the court cannot interfere with the decision 'simply because it would have given greater weight to the equality implications of the decision than did the decision maker'[208]. The battleground, therefore, is usually going to be whether the reviewing officer's PSED exercise was so bad that it actually amounted to a failure to comply with the duty, rather than whether the reviewing officer merely should have paid more attention to one aspect or another. This is a narrow distinction, but it can be an important one.

Wording of decisions

Particularly in homelessness challenges – where the PSED tends to form part of a written decision, rather than taking the form of a separate impact assessment – the courts have emphasised that compliance with the duty is a matter of substance, and not form[209]. In other words, the courts will tend to look at the broader contents of the decision, rather than parsing the reviewing officer's particular PSED phraseology. Judges will apply a 'fair, stand-back' reading to the decision[210].

This focus on the spirit, rather than the letter, of review decisions has led to an interesting outcome:

- On the one hand, a reviewing officer can comply with the PSED even if the duty is not specifically mentioned;

---

207 *Hackney LBC v Haque* [2017] PTSR 769, [2017] EWCA Civ 4, per Briggs LJ at [23].

208 *Hotak v Southwark LBC* [2016] AC 811, [2015] UKSC 30, per Lord Neuberger at [75], applying *R (Hurley & Moore) v Secretary of State for Business, Education & Skills* [2012] HRLR 13, [2012] EWHC 201 (Admin) per Elias LJ at [78].

209 See, e.g. *Hackney LBC v Haque* [2017] PTSR 769, [2017] EWCA Civ 4, per Briggs LJ at [21].

210 Ibid. at [50].

- On the other, a reviewing officer can breach the PSED even if they have cited the legislation and case law verbatim.

The first of those possibilities arises because the courts have held that it is possible for a decision-maker to comply with the PSED subconsciously: particularly where there is a close alignment between the requirements of the PSED and the requirements of the underlying statutory function, it is possible to comply with the equality duty despite not even knowing that it exists[211]. In practice, of course, while reviewing officers do not need to spell out their PSED responsibilities in every case, they tend to do so. The PSED is, after all, caught by the general statutory duty to give reasons for an adverse homelessness decision[212], and it is generally wise to set out the way in which the duty has been applied. Indeed, the Court of Appeal has said that it is 'reassuring to a court to see that a decision-maker has looked at specific aspects of the duty and can say what his/her response to it is'[213]. But even a review decision that totally fails to mention the PSED can survive a challenge.

The second possibility arises because explicitly spelling out the nature of the PSED will not assist a reviewing officer if there is an underlying error in approach. In *Lomax v Gosport*, for example, the Court of Appeal identified a breach of the PSED (the reviewing officer had compared the applicant to the wrong group of people), and rejected a submission that the decision was 'saved' by an explicit discussion of PSED issues[214]. Lewison LJ has also made the compelling point that the case law does not 'provid[e] a reviewing officer with a defensive ritual incantation', and 'the mere recitation of [case law] is no substitute for actually doing the job'[215].

211 *Hotak v Southwark LBC* [2016] AC 811, [2015] UKSC 30, per Lord Neuberger at [79].

212 *Hackney LBC v Haque* [2017] PTSR 769, [2017] EWCA Civ 4, per Briggs LJ at [48].

213 Ibid. per McCombe LJ at [63].

214 [2019] PTSR 167, [2018] EWCA Civ 1846, per Lewison LJ at [52].

215 *Kannan v Newham LBC* [2019] HLR 22, [2019] EWCA Civ 57, per Lewison LJ at [9, 24].

A review decision that faithfully sets out the law of the PSED – and many decisions do – is not immune from a successful challenge.

'In substance, with rigour, and with an open mind'

If they are not a defensive incantations or a high-minded mantras, what do phrases like this actually mean in practice?

In short, particularly in disability cases, reviewing officers have to grasp the nettle and acknowledge the hardship that the applicant would actually suffer without down-playing it. Attempts to skip over difficult facts are the most common form of breach in the reported cases. In *Lomax v Gosport* the Court of Appeal held that the reviewing officer had breached the PSED in that he had 'overlooked or downplayed the highly material and unchallenged evidence that her mental health was being positively damaged by remaining where she was; and the medical opinion that an immediate move was required' (original emphasis)[216]. In *Kannan v Newham*, similarly, it was a breach for the reviewing officer to 'down-grade' the appellant's symptoms, departing from the medical evidence without any real explanation. When reviewing officers try to shy away from inconvenient facts, the courts may treat this as a breach, even in cases where the decision is shrouded in the language of the case law.

It is important to note that the Court of Appeal has made it clear (albeit before *Lomax* and *Kannan*) that reviewing officers are not obliged to take the applicant's assertions about their impairments at face-value[217]. This reflects a broader principle of homelessness law[218]. But, if a reviewing officer wishes to reject or modify the applicant's account of their disability, they will need to give some rational explanation for doing so – particularly if it involves rejecting the evidence of the applicant's own

216 [2019] PTSR 167, [2018] EWCA Civ 1846, per Lewison LJ at [52]

217 *Hackney LBC v Haque* [2017] PTSR 769, [2017] EWCA Civ 4, per Briggs LJ at [45].

218 *R v Kensington & Chelsea RLBC v Cunha* (1989) 21 HLR 16.

medical professionals[219]. If there is any doubt or uncertainty – particularly in intentionality cases – the matter should be resolved in the applicant's favour[220]. Reviewing officers will need to be especially cautious about rejecting the applicant's case on disability in the PSED context, given the need for open-mindedness.

Not a 'box-ticking' exercise

The authorities repeatedly emphasise that the PSED is not an exercise in box-ticking[221]. This principle overlaps with the point about the wording of decisions: while courts and reviewing officers alike prefer to see the relevant legal principles set out in the review decision, merely including judicial phrases is not, itself, compliance with the PSED.

Defining & acknowledging disability

In disability cases, reviewing officers will often need (at the very least) to acknowledge that the applicant is under a disability. The need for a sharp focus on the existence and extent of a disability is probably the strongest and least contentious point to emerge from the various numbered lists set out in *Hotak*, *Haque* and *Lomax* (discussed under 'vulnerability' and 'suitability', above). If an applicant is caught by a relevant protected characteristic, there is simply no point from shying away from the fact.

Of course, in disability cases, proper compliance with the PSED will sometimes require reviewing officers to direct themselves correctly as to the legal definition of disability. As set out at '3.2 Triggering compliance' above, disability is a low threshold, and this can sometimes take reviewing officers by surprise.

---

219 *Guiste v Lambeth LBC* [2020] HLR 12, [2020] EWCA Civ 1758.

220 *R v Gravesham BC ex p Winchester* (1986) 18 HLR 207, per Simon Brown J at p.125, applying *R v Thurrock BC ex parte Williams* (1981-82) 1 HLR 128, per Phillips J at p.134.

221 See, e.g. *Hackney LBC v Haque* [2017] PTSR 769, [2017] EWCA Civ 4, per Briggs LJ at [22] and McCombe LJ at [63].

However, a review decision can survive a wrong self-direction as to disability, as long as there has otherwise been substantial compliance with the PSED. In *Haque* the reviewing officer had failed to consider whether the applicant was disabled within the strict definition of the Equality Act. But there was no breach of the PSED because, in substance, the reviewing officer had recognised that the applicant was disabled and treated him as such[222]. Similarly, in *McMahon*, Lewison LJ said: 'it is clear that a reviewing officer need not make findings about whether an applicant does or does not have a disability, or the precise effect of the PSED'[223]. In other words, there is no need to the reviewing officer to correctly apply the legal definition of disability – or even reach an explicit conclusion about whether there is a disability – as long as:

- The decision substantially treats the applicant as being under the protected characteristic of disability;
- The decision does not 'down-grade', unlawfully reject or fail to focus on the effects of the disability; and
- There has been substantive compliance with the PSED in other respects.

Taking relevant matters into account

The two most recent successful PSED homelessness authorities – *Lomax* and *Kannan* – have been characterised by the judge who decided them as cases where 'a review decision was vitiated by non-compliance with the PSED because of a failure to take specific features of the case into account'[224]. It is probably fair to say that the judgments in *Lomax* and *Kannan* are actually more nuanced and sophisticated than that, but it is

222 [2017] PTSR 769, [2017] EWCA Civ 4, per Briggs LJ at [49-50].

223 [2020] PTSR 1217, [2020] EWCA Civ 497, at [62]. See also [76-77] and [83-85].

224 *McMahon v Watford BC* [2020] PTSR 1217, [2020] EWCA Civ 497, per Lewison LJ at [64].

nevertheless clear that taking relevant matters into account is both a critical aspect of the PSED, and something that reviewing officers continue to get wrong.

In *Kannan* the reviewing officer 'misunderstood the thrust' of the council's own medical advice about the applicant's housing need, failed to take into account the duration of his occupation, and 'down-graded, without any explanation' the symptoms of his medical condition[225]. In *Lomax*, when assessing suitability, the reviewing officer had overlooked the harmful effects of the location of the accommodation[226]. The PSED – in particular its requirement for a 'sharp focus' – meant that the overlooking of those features had been unlawful, and perhaps made the argument more powerful that it would have been if argued as a simple public law failure to take relevant matters into account.

Correct comparators

In many types of homelessness dispute, the local authority will be comparing the applicant's particular situation to the situation of other people. In PSED cases this interacts with equality law, which seeks to protect people with protected characteristics in a rather specialised and technical manner. In short, local authorities cannot take the simple approach of comparing people with disabilities to other non-specified households. Instead, the comparison needs to be between people who have the particular needs that arise from the applicant's specific disability, and people who do not.

This became clear in the *Lomax* case. The applicant had particular disabilities, and her accommodation left her subject to harmful social isolation. The local authority – when it came to assess whether it was reasonable for her to remain in her accommodation – acted unlawfully by comparing her to 'the generality of persons on the council's waiting list': in other words, with people who did not have the same needs as the applicant, and who were not exposed to the same harm by remaining in

225 [2019] HLR 22, [2019] EWCA Civ 57, per Lewison LJ at [18, 20-22].

226 [2019] PTSR 167, [2018] EWCA Civ 1846, per Lewison LJ at [53-54].

their homes. It was submitted to the Court of Appeal that this actually amounted to unlawful discrimination, but the successful ground of appeal was that it was a breach of the PSED in carrying out the assessment of the adequacy of her home[227].

It would be unlawful for a local authority to conclude that a disabled applicant is 'in the same unfortunate boat' as everyone else that the council has to deal with, because that does not take account of the applicant's particular circumstances and their disability-related needs[228]. Instead, the local authority needs to 'have regard to duty to take steps to meet the different needs of a disabled person compared to those who are not disabled'. This involves asking whether the applicant's situation is out-of-the-ordinary, and may involve treating them more favourably[229].

Underlying discrimination

The County Court, when hearing a statutory homelessness appeal under section 204 of the Housing Act 1996, does not have the jurisdiction to consider allegations of Equality Act discrimination proper[230]. An applicant who wishes to bring a discrimination challenge will therefore have to bring a judicial review claim in the High Court, or a private law claim (probably in the County Court). If the applicant wishes to assert that the homelessness decision is vitiated by a breach of the PSED attaching to the fact that there has been actual discrimination, they would presumably have to stay any statutory homelessness appeal pending the resolution of the discrimination challenge, or possibly apply to transfer the homelessness appeal to the High Court on the basis that that the King's Bench Division would have the jurisdiction to hear both the

227 [2019] PTSR 167, [2018] EWCA Civ 1846, per Lewison LJ at [48].

228 Ibid. at [49]. See also *Kannan v Newham LBC* [2019] HLR 22, [2019] EWCA Civ 57, per Lewison LJ at [23].

229 Ibid. at [51].

230 *Adesotu v Lewisham LBC* [2019] 1 WLR 5637, [2019] EWCA Civ 1405.

statutory appeal and the discrimination judicial review[231], and could do so at the same time.

However, the more practical route is probably the sort of 'shadow boxing' that took place in *Lomax*. In that case the Court of Appeal heard submissions about whether the review decision amounted to an unlawful 'provision, criterion or practice' but did not decide the point[232]. A breach of the PSED was established instead, and the review decision was quashed on that basis. In many cases the court will not need to go as far as to decide whether there has been actual discrimination (and would not be able to do so). Because the PSED merely obliges the local authority to have due regard to the need to eliminate discrimination, a potentially or apparently discriminatory act may (as in *Lomax*) be sufficient.

3.5 Materiality

In homelessness law generally, the courts are subject to the well-known guidance in *Holmes-Moorhouse v Richmond-upon-Thames RLBC*[233] when it comes to the standard of scrutiny to be applied, and whether to grant a remedy in consequence of any error of law. The case is often summarised or quoted selectively, and homelessness practitioners would do well to frequently remind themselves of Lord Neuberger's rather evenly-balanced words in full:

> '46. The rights granted by Part VII of the 1996 Act to those claiming to be homeless or threatened with homelessness are based on humanitarian considerations, and this underlines the fact that any challenge to a review decision should be carefully considered by the county court to whom such challenges are directed. Given that the challenge in the

231 Equality Act 2010, section 113(3)(a); *Bankole-Jones v Watford BC* [2021] HLR 33, [2021] EWHC 3100 (Admin), per Mr Matthew Gullick at [7-9].

232 [2019] PTSR 167, [2018] EWCA Civ 1846, per Lewison LJ at [48].

233 [2009] 1 WLR 413, [2009] UKHL 9.

county court is treated as a first appeal, the responsibility on the judge considering the challenge is heavy, and, if he or she is satisfied that there is an error in the reasoning which undermines the basis upon which the decision was arrived at, then the decision should obviously be set aside.

47. However, a judge should not adopt an unfair or unrealistic approach when considering or interpreting such review decisions. Although they may often be checked by people with legal experience or qualifications before they are sent out, review decisions are prepared by housing officers, who occupy a post of considerable responsibility and who have substantial experience in the housing field, but they are not lawyers. It is not therefore appropriate to subject their decisions to the same sort of analysis as may be applied to a contract drafted by solicitors, to an Act of Parliament, or to a court's judgment.

48. Further, at least in my experience, and as this case exemplifies, review decisions generally set out the facts, the contentions, the analyses and the conclusions in some detail. To my mind, given the importance, particularly to the applicant, of the issues considered in review decisions, such fullness is to be strongly encouraged. However, as any lawyer knows, the more fully an opinion is expressed, the greater the opportunity for alleging mistakes of fact, errors of law, or inconsistencies. If the courts are too critical in their analyses of such decisions, it will tend to discourage reviewing officers from expressing themselves so fully.

49. In my view, it is therefore very important that, while circuit judges should be vigilant in ensuring that no applicant is wrongly deprived of benefits under Part VII of the 1996 Act because of any error on the part of the reviewing officer, it is equally important that an error which does not, on a fair analysis, undermine the basis of the decision, is not accepted as a reason for overturning the decision.

> 50. Accordingly, a benevolent approach should be adopted to the interpretation of review decisions. The court should not take too technical a view of the language used, or search for inconsistencies, or adopt a nit-picking approach, when confronted with an appeal against a review decision. That is not to say that the court should approve incomprehensible or misguided reasoning, but it should be realistic and practical in its approach to the interpretation of review decisions.
>
> 51. Further, as the present case shows, a decision can often survive despite the existence of an error in the reasoning advanced to support it. For example, sometimes the error is irrelevant to the outcome; sometimes it is too trivial (objectively, or in the eyes of the decision-maker) to affect the outcome; sometimes it is obvious from the rest of the reasoning, read as a whole, that the decision would have been the same notwithstanding the error; sometimes, there is more than one reason for the conclusion, and the error only undermines one of the reasons; sometimes, the decision is the only one which could rationally have been reached. In all such cases, the error should not (save, perhaps, in wholly exceptional circumstances) justify the decision being quashed'.

This is important for present purposes because Lord Neuberger himself, in *Hotak*, gave the hint of a suggestion that his guidance might not be applied quite as strictly in PSED cases. At [79] he explained: 'I said [in *Holmes-Moorhouse*] that a "benevolent" and "not too technical" approach to section 202 review letters was appropriate, that one should not "search for inconsistencies", and that immaterial errors should not have an invalidating effect. I strongly maintain those views, <u>but</u> they now have to be read in the light of the contents of para 78 above in a case where the equality duty is engaged'[234] (emphasis added). Paragraph 78 contained

[234] [2016] AC 811, [2015] UKSC 30, per Lord Neuberger at [79].

Lord Neuberger's warning against 'high-minded mantras' and his call for a 'sharp focus' on the PSED.

It should be noted that the Supreme Court has, more recently, applied the *Holmes-Moorhouse* principle in a PSED case in its original and unmodified state[235]. But, equally notably, the Supreme Court was explicit that it was not concerned, in that case, with determining the issue of standards of judicial scrutiny[236]. It may still be a matter of debate whether Lord Neuberger meant that the *Holmes-Moorhouse* principle is somehow tempered in PSED challenges.

As ever, the question of materiality and remedy are highly case-specific. Applicants' representatives will wish to cite the many high authorities in which the courts have highlighted the importance of the PSED. The Court of Appeal has pointed out that leading judges have stressed its importance, holding that '[i]nattention to [the equality duty] is both unlawful and bad government'[237]. Similarly, in the leading PSED case of *Bracking*, Elias LJ said: '[i]t seems to me that if a decision is reached without due regard to the PSED then it is an unlawful decision and, subject to any overarching discretionary features, the decision should be quashed'[238]. Local authority lawyers, for their part, will cite Lewison LJ's point that the PSED is not 'a disciplinary stick with which to beat [reviewing officers]'.

---

235 *Poshteh v Kensington & Chelsea RLBC* [2017] AC 624, [2017] UKSC 36, per Lord Carnwath at [38-39]. See also *McMahon v Watford BC* [2020] PTSR 1217, [2020] EWCA Civ 497, per Lewison LJ at [16-17].

236 Ibid. (*Poshteh*) at [42].

237 *R (C) v Secretary of State for Justice* [2009] QB 657, [2008] EWCA Civ 882, per Buxton LJ at [49].

238 *Bracking v Secretary of State for Work & Pensions* [2014] EqLR 60, [2013] EWCA Civ 1345, per McCombe LJ at [69].

3.6 Representations

In theory, the most important aspect of representations in homelessness cases is to simply provide the local authority with the information that it needs in order to trigger compliance with the PSED. It is, after all, supposed to be a proactive duty on the public authority, which bears the duty of inquiry to equip itself with the information that it needs to make a fair decision.

In practice, however, the more that can be spelled out to the local authority, the better. Given the prohibition on (irrationally) rejecting the applicant's case (see '3.4 Aspects of compliance; in substance, with rigour, and with an open mind', above), it is normally in the applicant's interest to put their position on record, and to assist the reviewing officer in complying with their duty as much as possible. In general, therefore, representations should include:

- The assertion that the applicant is under a protected characteristic;
- An explanation of the nature of the protected characteristic;
- An explanation of the extent of the protected characteristic;
- An explanation of any particular needs arising from the protected characteristic; and
- How, in specific terms, the effects of the protected characteristic have a bearing upon the underlying dispute.

Medical or supporting evidence should be included where possible. Where it is not possible, it may be worth pointing out that the PSED imposes an 'enhanced' duty of inquiry (see '3.3 Inquiries', above), and identifying any evidence that the local authority itself ought to collect.

Practitioners may be concerned that spelling out the PSED in too-precise terms will allow cynical reviewing officers to simply appear to comply and reach an adverse decision anyway, robbing the applicant of a viable ground of appeal. But there are two responses to that. First, as set out at '3.4 Aspects of compliance; wording of decision' above, by merely explaining the nature of the PSED, applicants' lawyers are not going to "provid[e] a reviewing officer with a defensive ritual incantation'. The courts will generally look at the substance, not the form, of the decision, and if there has been a breach notwithstanding the inclusion PSED-type language in the decision, this will be apparent. Second, as a matter of experience, the courts are likely to be more receptive to PSED arguments where there have been sincere efforts to invite the local authority to comply, and less receptive where the PSED is sprung on the local authority at the appeal stage. Even where they fail to change the reviewing officer's mind, good, thorough representations are always helpful when cases are argued on appeal, and are hardly ever a hindrance.

3.7 Evidence

While the courts have repeatedly said that a statutory homelessness appeal (being akin to judicial review) is not usually an appropriate forum for fact-finding, and that <u>live</u> evidence will be admitted exceptionally rarely[239], that is not to say that there is no place for written evidence, even if it post-dates the decision under appeal.

Indeed, the courts have been fairly clear that evidence is often necessary in cases concerning alleged procedural failings[240]. Given that the PSED is, by its nature, a process duty, there are bound to be PSED cases in which post-decision evidence is appropriate. These might include, for example, cases where the applicant files evidence of what the reviewing officer <u>would</u> have found if adequate inquiries had been made: perhaps further medical evidence, or direct evidence from the applicant about the nature or extent of their disability. Indeed, sometimes it may be entirely

239 *Bubb v Wandsworth LBC* [2012] PTSR 1011, [2011] EWCA Civ 1285, per Lord Neuberger MR at [21, 25-26].

240 *Richmond-upon-Thames RLBC v Kubicek* (unrep.) [2012] EWHC 3292, per Leggatt J at [18-20].

necessary to adduce evidence in order to satisfy the court that the appeal should not be dismissed on a *Holmes-Moorhouse* or materiality basis.

For example, in *Pieretti*[241], the judgment contains slightly speculative references to the applicant's disability and its potential effects. It might have been helpful, if the court were deciding a *Pieretti*-type case today, for the parties to adduce some evidence about whether the connection between the disability and intentionally was a genuine possibility, or merely speculative. Equally, however, the Court of Appeal has expressed some concern about evidence in a PSED case that went beyond what was strictly necessary to illuminate the point or law, or to justify the grant of a remedy[242], and evidence should be limited to what is needed.

Unless the opposing party challenges the contents of a witness statement – and assuming that the evidence is not 'manifestly wrong' – the court ought to accept the evidence as being true[243].

3.8 Where next?

There are bound to be more homelessness cases concerning the PSED. In the summer of 2022 the Court of Appeal granted permission to bring a second appeal in a case concerning intentionality[244] – which is

241 [2011] PTSR 565, [2010] EWCA Civ 1104.

242 *Biden v Waverley BC* [2022] PTSR 1056, [2022] EWCA Civ 442, per Macur LJ at [38], applying *Cramp v Hastings BC* [2005] HLR 48, [2005] EWCA Civ 1005, per Brooke LJ at [71].

243 *R (Safeer) v Secretary of State for the Home Department* [2018] EWCA Civ 2518, per Davies LJ at [16-19] (applied in the homelessness context in, e.g., *Morocho v Haringey LBC* (unrep.) County Court at Central London, 27th May 2022, per HHJ Roberts at [26, 28] – the author may be contacted for a copy of the judgment).

244 'Court of Appeal to hear case on housing authority duties to comply with Public Sector Equality Duty', *Local Government Lawyer*, 16th June 2022 (localgovernmentlawyer.co.uk). Many thanks to Sonia Birdee of Garden

something of a missing link in the authorities. 2022 also saw the first homelessness case concerning gender reassignment as a protected characteristic[245].

It will also be interesting to see whether any policy challenges are brought, within the jurisdiction of statutory homelessness appeals. The Supreme Court has indicated that it is possible – indeed, sometimes it is more practical – for an applicant to challenge the legality of the policy in statutory appeal proceedings, rather than by judicial review[246].

Some obvious possibilities spring to mind. In a high-profile challenge against Birmingham City Council, for example, the Court of Appeal held that Birmingham's practice of operating a waiting list that failed to differentiate between households with disability needs and households without such needs amounted to a failure to comply with the PSED[247]. It may be possible – particularly in suitability-type appeals – to include a challenge to a temporary accommodation policy or a placement policy that fails to comply with the PSED in a similar way. This might relate to disability needs, or potentially to sex: given that the Supreme Court has accepted (without the point being contentious) that the 'benefits cap' has a disproportionate impact on women, a policy that displaces benefits-capped families would presumably have to demonstrate fairly rigorous compliance with the PSED[248].

Otherwise, while we have now seen a number of 'inherently close alignment'-type cases, judicial guidance is lacking when it comes to issues

---

Court North Chambers, who informed the author that the case (*Chalmers v Nottingham CC*) was settled after permission was granted.

245 *Biden v Waverley BC* [2022] PTSR 1056, [2022] EWCA Civ 442.

246 *Nzolameso v Westminster CC* [2015] 2 All ER 942, [2015] UKSC 22, per Baroness Hale at [41].

247 *R (Elkundi) v Birmingham CC* [2022] QB 604, [2022] EWCA Civ 601, per Lewis LJ at [114].

248 *R (SG) v Secretary of State for Work & Pensions* [2015] 1 WLR 1449, [2015] UKSC 16, per Lord Reed at [2].

where there is less elision between the nature of the decision under review and the performance of the PSED. While guidance is lacking, there are bound to be challenges.

CHAPTER FOUR

ALLOCATIONS & HOUSING JUDICIAL REVIEWS

4.1 Context: a troubling legacy

The Race Relations Act 1976 was a signal event in the evolution of equality and anti-discrimination law. One if its major aspects was the establishment of the statutory body that preceded the Equality and Human Rights Commission, the Commission for Racial Equality. The CRE began its work in the 1970s by exposing several local authorities' unequal treatment of different racial groups in housing allocations decisions[249]. Some of this social engineering was carried out on the patrician basis that housing schemes would be more harmonious if estates weren't racially 'mixed'[250], while others took the opposite (but equally patrician) standpoint that recent migrants should be dispersed rather than concentrated in established minoritised communities[251].

It is tempting to cast this as a historical aberration, which has long since been overcome. But it is a troubling fact that just 11 of the 68 residents of the Grenfell Tower who died in 2017 fire were white[252]. Just as stark

249 See, e.g. Sam Wetherell (2020), *Foundations*, Princeton University Press, p.116.

250 John Boughton (2019), *Municipal Dreams*, Verso, p.212-214.

251 Birmingham, for example, had a policy that no more than one in six tenants in a given building could be black, with an aim to dispersing black tenants into white suburbs. See Richard Vinen (2022), *Second City: Birmingham and the Forging of Modern Britain*, Allen Lane, ch.9 fn.32.

252 While there were 72 recorded deaths, four of those were visitors rather than residents. Speech by Leslie Thomas KC, July 2021, cited in Peter Apps, 'The Grenfell Tower Fire Was Part of Britain's Colonial Legacy', *Tribune* 21st September 2021.

is the fact that the tower also housed 37 residents with disabilities that prevented them from escaping unaided, of whom 15 were killed on the night of the fire. And with the housing crisis and the gender pay gap both intensifying at the same time, by spring 2022 there was not a single region in England where the average rent was affordable to a single woman on median earnings[253]. The need for effective tools against systemic discrimination in allocations and housing management decisions is almost as sharp as it ever was.

This chapter is mainly concerned with allocations judicial reviews, which is the form of housing dispute in which (apart from possession claims and homelessness appeals) the PSED has most commonly been litigated. But the relevant principles – particularly when read with chapter 3 – should be equally applicable in other housing policy challenges (for example challenges to homelessness strategies or inadequate levels of service provision) and individual challenges (for example homelessness judicial reviews and housing management matters).

4.2 When to comply

In theory – and as a matter of best practice – local housing authorities must comply with the PSED before a policy is adopted, or a decision is reached. The Court of Appeal has explained that the purpose of the old Race Relations Act duty was to require public authorities to give 'advance consideration' to issues of discrimination[254], and – in another case – that

[253] Vicky Spratt, 'Women face growing gender housing gap as rents, house prices and wage inequality spiral', *i News* 15th March 2022.

[254] *R (Elias) v Secretary of State for Defence* [2006] 1 WLR CA, [2006] EWCA Civ 1293, per Arden LJ at [272-274]. This point in *Elias* has subsequently been applied in e.g: *R (Kaur & Shah) v Ealing LBC* [2008] EWHC 2062 (Admin) per Moses LJ at [23]; *R (C) v Secretary of State for Justice* [2008] EWHC 171 (Admin) per Muarice Kay LJ at [37, 39]; the appeal in *R (C)* [2009] QB 657, [2008] EWCA Civ 882, per Buxton LJ at [49]; *R (Brown) v Secretary of State for Work & Pensions* [2009] PTSR 1506, [2008] EWHC 3158 (Admin), per Scott Baker and Aikens LJJ at [88]; *R (Hurley & Moore) v Secretary of State for Business, Education & Skills* [2012] HRLR 13, [2012]

compliance must take place 'not as a rearguard action following a concluded decision but as an essential preliminary'[255]. The need for advance compliance has been specifically cited in the allocations context[256], with the High Court emphasising that part of the purpose of the PSED is that local authorities should be alert to the possibility of unintended consequences on groups with protected characteristics[257].

In a challenge to a homelessness strategy, it was held that the PSED (in combination with the provisions of the Homelessness Act 2002 and section 11 of the Children Act 2004) required the local authority to 'think <u>in advance</u> who would need its services, how many would have disability needs and what they [the local authority] would need to do to meet those needs' (emphasis added), and to 'be proactive in ensuring that they have available to them housing that will need the needs of families with disabled children'[258].

However, there are two important caveats to that principle. First, the PSED is a continuing duty[259]. This means that compliance does not take place once and for all, when the local authority is formulating a policy or

EWHC 201 (Admin), per Elias LJ at [71-72]; and – perhaps most authoritatively – *Bracking v Secretary of State for Work & Pensions* [2014] EqLR 60, [2013] EWCA Civ 1345, per McCombe LJ at [26(4)].

255 *R (BAPIO Action Ltd) v Secretary of State for the Home Department* [2007] EWCA Civ 1139, per Sedley LJ at [3].

256 *R (Nur) v Birmingham CC (no.1)* [2021] HLR 23, [2020] EWHC 3526 (Admin), per David Lock QC at [47-48].

257 *R (Nur) v Birmingham CC (no.2)* [2021] HLR 41, [2020] EWHC 1138 (Admin), per David Lock QC at [132].

258 *R (Bell) v Lambeth LBC* [2022] HLR 45, [2022] EWHC 2008 (Admin), per Hill J at [70, 116].

259 *R (Brown) v Secretary of State for Work & Pensions* [2009] PTSR 1506, [2008] EWHC 3158 (Admin), per Scott Baker and Aikens LJJ at [95], applied in *Bracking v Secretary of State for Work & Pensions* [2014] EqLR 60, [2013] EWCA Civ 1345, per McCombe LJ at [26(5)(v)]. For application in the allocations context, see *R (Nur) v Birmingham CC (no.2)* [2021] HLR 41, [2020] EWHC 1138 (Admin), per David Lock QC at [13].

decision. Instead, the duty requires councils to comply with the duty at every stage of the proceedings and in light of any judgment[260].

Second, while the point may not be entirely settled, it appears that the effect of the Court of Appeal's decision in *TM v Metropolitan* is that a breach of the PSED at an early stage can in principle be 'remedied' by later compliance[261]. Allocations judicial reviews lend themselves well to becoming 'then and now' challenges, in which the claimant begins by alleging that the policy was formulated in breach of the PSED, but as the proceedings evolve they may also find themselves critiquing any subsequent attempt by the local authority to assess or justify the policy retrospectively[262]. *TM* suggests that where a local authority has complied with the PSED late, that does not mean that there was never a breach: instead, it means that the initial breach may no longer have any continuing consequences, which will inform the court's decision as to whether to grant any remedy in consequence of the breach.

However, local authorities would be best advised to comply with the PSED at the outset: partly because this would achieve the statutory aim of ensuring that their decisions are informed by a 'full appraisal' of equality issues; and partly because it would avoid complex and risky disputes about whether later attempts at compliance were an exercise in

---

260 See e.g. *R (H) v Ealing LBC (EHRC intervening)* [2018] PTSR 541, [2017] EWCA Civ 1127, per Sir Terence Etherton MR at [114-117].

261 [2022] 1 WLR 2161, [2021] EWCA Civ 1890, per Nugee LJ at [43-47]. See also Green LJ at [62-64]. Strictly speaking, this point was decided *obiter*. See also *R (H) v Ealing LBC (EHRC intervening)* [2018] PTSR 541, [2017] EWCA Civ 1127, per Sir Terence Etherton MR at [114-117], an earlier case in which the Court of Appeal appeared to accept that it was notionally possibly to comply with the PSED during the course of proceedings, although the local authority had not done so on the facts of that case.

262 *R (Rowley) v Minister for the Cabinet Office* [2022] 1 WLR 1189, [2021] EWHC 2108 (Admin), at [10]. For an example in the allocations context, see See e.g. *R (H) v Ealing LBC (EHRC intervening)* [2018] PTSR 541, [2017] EWCA Civ 1127, per Sir Terence Etherton MR at [114-117].

'confirmation bias', which the courts may treat with greater scrutiny[263]. And the later the attempt, the more difficult it may be to satisfy the court that there has been compliance: as the Court of Appeal said of the risk of confirmation bias in *TM v Metropolitan*: 'this perhaps particularly so in the case of litigation, where costs have already been incurred and the incentive to pursue the proceedings to a successful conclusion can be very high'[264].

4.3 Triggering compliance

In summary, and assuming that it is relevant, local authorities will be required to comply with the PSED:

- Where the need to comply is obvious;
- Where the claimant invites them to consider the PSED; and/or
- Where the evidence raises a 'real possibility' that there may be a relevant equality issue.

The PSED only arises where the applicant is under a protected characteristic which is in some way relevant to any particular aspect(s) of housing rights that the local authority is required to determine in a given case[265]. In other words, the PSED does not arise in every case, but only

---

263 *R (Ward & Gullu) v Hillingdon LBC* [2019] PTSR 1738, [2019] EWCA Civ 692, per Lewison LJ at [76]. See also See also: *TM v Metropolitan HT* [2022] 1 WLR 2161, [2021] EWCA Civ 1890, per Nugee LJ at [39] and Green LJ at [65] (on 'confirmation bias'); *R (H) v Ealing LBC (EHRC intervening)* [2018] PTSR 541, [2017] EWCA Civ 1127, per Sir Terence Etherton MR at [114-117] (the Court of Appeal rejecting an *ex post facto* witness statement as not amounting to compliance with the PSED).

264 [2022] 1 WLR 2161, [2021] EWCA Civ 1890, per Nugee LJ at [39.] See also Green LJ's comments at [65].

265 *Pieretti v Enfield LBC* [2011] PTSR 565, [2010] EWCA Civ 1104, per Wilson LJ at [35-36], applied in *Hotak v Southwark LBC* [2016] AC 811, [2015] UKSC 30, per Lord Neuberger at [77]. In the allocations context see

where some equality aspect is relevant. Even though every applicant will have a number of protected characteristics, the PSED can often be safely ignored. For example, if an applicant who brings a challenge is a member of the Church of England, it is difficult to conceive of a forceful argument that the average local authority must focus sharply on religion or belief when reaching an allocations decision or drafting an allocations scheme.

In other housing law contexts, the Court of Appeal has been clear that compliance is triggered not only where it has been established that the applicant has a protected characteristic, but also where some feature of the evidence presents a 'real possibility' that the applicant has a relevant protected characteristic[266].

More directly relevant to allocations law, though, is the situation where an applicant raises a relevant protected characteristic after an allocations scheme has been formulated, and which the local authority had not considered. This arose in *R (Ward & Gullu) v Hillingdon.* Lewison LJ held that the PSED does not oblige local authorities to assess the impact of an allocations scheme on 'every conceivable group that shares a protected characteristic', and gave the examples of 'Native Americans or Aboriginal Australians' as groups that would not tend to need specific consideration in advance. If the local authority has acted 'reasonably and in all good faith' and had given 'adequate thought' to which groups ought to be considered, there would not be a breach of the PSED if a particular group was missed[267].

But, equally, there will be a breach of the PSED from the point at which an applicant raises a relevant protected characteristic which the local authority has, in all good conscience, missed. The local authority would then be obliged to 'at least consider' the impact of the allocations scheme

---

R (Nur) v Birmingham CC (no.2) [2021] HLR 41, [2020] EWHC 1138 (Admin), per David Lock QC at [148].

266 *Pieretti v Enfield LBC* [2011] PTSR 565, [2010] EWCA Civ 1104, per Wilson LJ at [35].

267 *R (Ward & Gullu) v Hillingdon LBC* [2019] PTSR 1738, [2019] EWCA Civ 692, per Lewison LJ at [72, 81].

on that group (in other words, to comply with the PSED in the manner described in '4.5 Aspects of compliance', below). Thus the PSED could be triggered before litigation is anticipated, at the pre-action stage, or (as in the Hillingdon case) during the litigation itself[268].

When it comes to disability, the Court of Appeal has said (in another housing law context, homelessness) applicants themselves do not need to explicitly raise disability. In *Pieretti* Wilson LJ said that the PSED is designed to foster a culture of greater awareness of disability-related issues, 'including the fact that a disabled person may not be adept at proclaiming his disability'[269]. This principle modified the earlier judicial thinking that homelessness appeals should generally be constrained to issues that were either obvious, or had been specifically raised by the applicant. This, of course, does not preclude an applicant or their advisers from raising disability or the PSED in representations as a way of triggering or ensuring compliance, and applicants would often be well-advised to be as clear and explicit about the PSED as possible, even where the evidence had passed that 'real possibility' test.

It is worth noting that the threshold for 'disability' is low. Section 6 of the Equality Act 2010, read with section 212, has the effect that a person is under the protected characteristic of disability if they have a physical or mental impairment which has an adverse effect on their ability to carry out normal day-to-day activities, and the effect is more than minor or trivial. Thus the PSED has a very light trigger: an applicant must merely present a 'real possibility' of a condition that has a 'more than minimal' effect on their daily living, assuming that the disability is in some way relevant. In one allocations judicial review, the local authority breached the PSED (in part) by adopting a different definition of disability, and

268 Ibid. at [74].

269 *Pieretti v Enfield LBC* [2011] PTSR 565, [2010] EWCA Civ 1104, per Wilson LJ at [28].

by failing to evaluate the consequences that arose from using its own definition[270].

There are three medical conditions that always constitute disabilities, regardless of severity: cancer, multiple sclerosis and HIV[271]. There are also a number of conditions which regulations exclude from the definition of disability. These include substance addiction, tendency to start fires, tendency to steal, tendency to commit physical or sexual abuse, exhibitionism and voyeurism[272]. There is also statutory guidance on the definition of disability, which contains some useful practical examples and case studies[273]. This guidance is particularly useful where there is an overlap between excluded conditions and other disabilities, for example where mental ill-health gives rise to substance misuse. Courts <u>must</u> take that guidance into account where it is relevant[274].

If it is unclear whether the PSED applies, or whether it is relevant, the duty itself may oblige local authorities to carry out further inquiries to reach an answer, so that they make their decision from a properly-informed perspective[275].

---

270 *R (H) v Ealing LBC (EHRC intervening)* [2018] PTSR 541, [2017] EWCA Civ 1127, per Sir Terence Etherton MR at [115].

271 Equality Act 2010, schedule 1 para 6.

272 Equality Act 2010 (Disability) Regulations 2010, regs. 3-4.

273 'Equality Act 2010 Guidance: Guidance on matters to be taken into account in determining questions relating to the definition of disability', Office for Disability Issues.

274 Equality Act 2010, schedule 1 para 12. The guidance is issued pursuant to sub-section 6(5) of the Act.

275 *R (Hurley & Moore) v Secretary of State for Business, Education & Skills* [2012] HRLR 13, [2012] EWHC 201 (Admin) per Elias LJ at [89-90]. In the allocations context, see *R (Ward & Gullu) v Hillingdon LBC* [2019] PTSR 1738, [2019] EWCA Civ 692, per Lewison LJ at [71], on the need for the decision-maker to be 'properly informed'. *Hurley & Moore* was also cited in the homelessness context in *Hotak v Southwark LBC* [2016] AC 811, [2015] UKSC 30, per Lord Neuberger at [77], which was, in turn, cited in an

Presumably, where it has been established that an applicant's condition does not meet the definition of disability, the PSED (insofar as it is relevant to disability) falls away[276].

4.4 Evidence

Presumably – although it does not appear to have been tested – section 136 of the Equality Act 2010 applies to PSED challenges in housing judicial reviews. This means that the landlord will bear the burden of proving that it has complied with the PSED, if there are facts from which the court could decide (in the absence of any other explanation) that the local authority has not complied. In other words, the burden of proof shifts to the defendant when there is a *prima facie* case of a non-compliance.

While it is not a strict legal requirement of the PSED itself, the courts have repeatedly pointed out that keeping records of compliance is 'good practice' or an 'important evidential element in demonstrating the discharge of the duty'[277]. Whether or not such records are produced,

allocations case: *R (C) v Islington LBC* [2017] HLR 32, [2017] EWHC 1288 (Admin) per Baker J at [100]. See '4.5 Aspects of compliance; inquiries' (below).

[276] See e.g. *Swan HA v Gill* [2014] HLR 18, [2013] EWCA Civ 1556, a possession case.

[277] *R (Brown) v Secretary of State for Work & Pensions* [2009] PTSR 1506, [2008] EWHC 3158 (Admin), per Scott Baker and Aikens LJJ at [96]; *Bracking v Secretary of State for Work & Pensions* [2014] EqLR 60, [2013] EWCA Civ 1345, per McCombe LJ at [26(2)]. *Bracking* was cited in the first-instance decision in *R (H) v Ealing LBC* [2016] PTSR 1546, [2016] EWHC 481 (Admin), per HHJ Waksman QC at [106]. The judge said the PSED imposes a 'heavy burden on public authorities in discharging the PSED and they must ensure that there is evidence available to demonstrate the discharge of this duty'. On appeal, his decision concerning the PSED was upheld in part: [2018] PTSR 541, [2017] EWCA Civ 1127.

there must at least be some evidence of what the local authority did to discharge the duty, which must go beyond mere generalities[278].

A practice has developed among public authorities of demonstrating compliance with the PSED through some form of written impact assessment. This dates back to the 'racial equality impact assessments' that used to be carried out to demonstrate compliance with the old Race Relations Act duty. But it should be emphasised that merely preparing an impact assessment is not, itself, compliance with the PSED. Such an assessment is only evidence, which records the steps that the decision-maker has taken when complying (or attempting to comply) with the duty.

Indeed, the courts have been clear that there is no need for a formal equality impact assessment[279], and it is settled law that compliance with the PSED does not need to take any specific form[280]. In the allocations context, for example, the courts have been prepared to scrutinise both the allocations scheme itself[281], and the surrounding circumstances[282], in assessing whether there has been compliance in the absence of an equality impact assessment.

But, whatever the format of the evidence, the courts have explicitly said that that compliance means showing a 'proper and conscientious focus

---

[278] *R (Good Law Project) v Prime Minister* [2022] ACD 50, [2022] EWHC 298 (Admin), per Singh LJ at [112, 114, 116].

[279] *R (Elkundi) v Birmingham CC* [2022] QB 604, [2022] EWCA Civ 601, per Lewis LJ at [114]; *R (C) v Islington LBC* [2017] HLR 32, [2017] EWHC 1288 (Admin) per Baker J at [104].

[280] *R (Sheakh) v Lambeth LBC* [2022] PTSR 1315, [2022] EWCA Civ 457, per Sir Keith Lindblom SPT, Males & Laing LJJ at [10].

[281] *R (C) v Islington LBC* [2017] HLR 32, [2017] EWHC 1288 (Admin) per Baker J at [104].

[282] *R (Elkundi) v Birmingham CC* [2022] QB 604, [2022] EWCA Civ 601, per Lewis LJ at [114].

on the statutory criteria'[283], and that there is a difference between loose, general regard to equality issues more broadly (which does not amount to compliance with the PSED) and having specific regard to the section 149 criteria (which does)[284]. In other words, there is a clear need to show conscientious compliance with the PSED[285], and (often) this is most easily demonstrated by an equality impact assessment.

Given the need for advance compliance, any equality impact assessment that was carried out while preparing an allocations scheme will be of obvious interest to the court[286]. But an original, contemporaneous assessment may not be determinative: partly because (as set out at '4.3 Triggering compliance', above) there will be cases where a particular group or issue was initially missed; and partly because there may have been some staff turnover, and the PSED falls upon the decision-maker personally[287].

Where witness evidence is produced, either as an alternative or a supplement to an equality impact assessment, local authorities will need

---

283 *Bracking v Secretary of State for Work & Pensions* [2014] EqLR 60, [2013] EWCA Civ 1345, per McCombe LJ at [26(8)(i)], citing Elias LJ in *Hurley & Moore* at [78].

284 *R (Meaney) v Harlow DC* (unrep.) [2009] EWHC 559 (Admin) per Davis J at [84], cited with approval in *R (Sheakh) v Lambeth LBC* [2022] PTSR 1315, [2022] EWCA Civ 457, per Sir Keith Lindblom SPT, Males & Laing LJJ at [12]. See also *R (MA) v Secretary of State for Work & Pensions* [2016] 1 WLR 4550, [2016] UKSC 58, per Lord Toulson at [68].

285 See, e.g. *R (Nur) v Birmingham CC (no.1)* [2021] HLR 23, [2021] EWHC 3526 (Admin.) per David Lock QC at [47].

286 *R (C) v Islington LBC* [2017] HLR 32, [2017] EWHC 1288 (Admin) per Baker J at [101-102].

287 *Bracking v Secretary of State for Work & Pensions* [2014] EqLR 60, [2013] EWCA Civ 1345, per McCombe LJ at [26(3)]. In *R (Nur) v Birmingham CC (no.1)* [2021] HLR 23, [2021] EWHC 3526 (Admin.) per David Lock QC at [49] (an allocations case) evidence from a member of staff about why she believed the public authority might have taken a particular approach did not demonstrate compliance with the PSED.

to learn the lesson of the Ealing allocations challenge and lead evidence that actually demonstrates adequate compliance with the PSED[288]. It should also be noted that the courts will not necessarily take local authorities' witness evidence at face-value, notwithstanding the general principle that judicial review courts should be slow to refuse to accept evidence that has not been challenged by an application for cross-examination[289].

4.5 Aspects of compliance

In allocations challenges concerning the PSED, the relevant 'functions' for the purposes of section 149(1) are the setting up and maintaining of the allocation scheme[290].

As in all PSED cases, a PSED point is a challenge to the decision-making process, and not the outcome[291]. A claimant raising the PSED is only ever saying 'the local authority has not thought about this carefully

---

[288] *R (H) v Ealing LBC (EHRC intervening)* [2018] PTSR 541, [2017] EWCA Civ 1127, per Sir Terence Etherton MR at [115]. See also *R (Nur) v Birmingham CC (no.1)* [2021] HLR 23, [2021] EWHC 3526 (Admin.) per David Lock QC at [49].

[289] *R (Nur) v Birmingham CC (no.2)* [2021] HLR 41, [2020] EWHC 1138 (Admin), per David Lock QC at [67-79], considering and applying the evidential principles set out in *R (Safeer) v Secretary of State for the Home Department* [2018] EWCA Civ 2581 and *R (Fisher) v North Derbyshire Health Authority* [1997] EWHC Admin 675.

[290] *R (H) v Ealing LBC* [2016] PTSR 1546, [2016] EWHC 481 (Admin), per HHJ Waksman QC at [107].

[291] See, e.g. *R (Rowley) v Minister for the Cabinet Office* [2022] 1 WLR 1189, [2021] EWHC 2108 (Admin), per Fordham J at [39]. In the allocations context see *R (Gullu) v Hillingdon LBC* [2019] HLR 4, [2018] EWHC 1937, per Mostyn J at [43].

enough', rather than 'the local authority has reached the wrong decision'. But this does not diminish its importance[292].

The statutory criteria

The starting point for complying with the PSED is the words of the statute itself. Despite the many judicial statements summarising the spirit and purpose of the PSED, there is no better guide for local authorities (or applicants or judges scrutinising PSED compliance) than the primary legislation. Indeed, the courts have explicitly said that judicial decisions describing the PSED are merely 'glosses' which 'are no substitute for the statute'[293].

Section 149 therefore provides an essential checklist. Both parties should ensure that that the local authority has demonstrated a proper, conscientious focus on:

- The possibility that there has been discrimination, harassment (in the strict statutory sense, i.e. 'unwanted conduct' relevant to a protected characteristic)[294], victimisation (also in the strict statutory sense, i.e. subjecting someone to a detriment in retaliation for relying on their Equality Act protections[295]), and/or other prohibited conduct such as a failure to make reasonable adjustments[296];

---

292 *R (Bridges) v Chief Constable of South Wales Police* [2020] 1 WLR 5064, [2020] EWCA Civ 1058, per Sir Terence Etherton MR, Dame Victoria Sharp PQBD & Singh LJ at [176].

293 *R (Sheakh) v Lambeth LBC* [2022] PTSR 1315, [2022] EWCA Civ 457, per Sir Keith Lindblom SPT, Males & Laing LJJ at [13].

294 Equality Act 2010, section 26.

295 Equality Act 2010, section 27.

296 Breach of the reasonable adjustment duty is, strictly speaking, a form of discrimination rather than 'any other conduct': Equality Act 2010, section 21(2).

- The need to advance equality of opportunity, which includes having regard to the need to:
    - Remove or minimise disadvantages that people with protected characteristics face;
    - Take steps to meet the different needs of people with protected characteristics;
    - Encourage people with protected characteristics to participate in public life and societal activity;
- The need to foster good relations, which includes having regard to the need to:
    - Tackle prejudice;
    - Promote understanding;
- The particular needs of people with disabilities; and
- Whether it may be appropriate to treat tenants with protected characteristics more favourably than others.

In essence, and where appropriate, compliance with the PSED involves considering those matters 'in substance, with rigour and with an open mind'[297].

<u>The key principles</u>

While the courts have been very clear that the PSED is highly context-specific[298], the leading homelessness authorities have been cited an

[297] *R (H) v Ealing LBC (EHRC intervening)* [2018] PTSR 541, [2017] EWCA Civ 1127, per Sir Terence Etherton MR at [111].

[298] *Powell v Dacorum BC* [2019] HLR 21, [2019] EWCA Civ 23, per McCombe LJ at [44].

applied in the allocations field[299]. This, presumably, means that principles set out in the Supreme Court's decision in *Hotak v Southwark* and the Court of Appeal's decision in *Hackney v Haque* have a great deal of relevance in many allocations disputes (those decisions are discussed under 'vulnerability' and 'suitability' at '3.4 Aspects of compliance' above).

The key principles of the PSED in allocations challenges are therefore as follows:

- The aim of the PSED is to place equality issues at the centre of public decision-making;
- The PSED is a 'due regard' duty, and is a matter of substance rather than form;
- The duty must be carried out in substance, with rigour and with an open mind and is not a 'box-ticking' exercise;
- It is not a duty to give any specific weight to the statutory criteria, and the court cannot interfere on the basis that it would have given more weight to a particular matter.

Consequences of scheme

It is clear from the reported cases that the PSED in allocations disputes is particularly concerned with considering the impact of allocations provisions upon groups with protected characteristics. This stems from the more general case law about the need to assess the impact of any given policy or decision[300], but the point has been authoritatively applied in

[299] *R (H) v Ealing LBC (EHRC intervening)* [2018] PTSR 541, [2017] EWCA Civ 1127, per Sir Terence Etherton MR at [111-112].

[300] See, e.g. *Bracking v Secretary of State for Work & Pensions* [2014] EqLR 60, [2013] EWCA Civ 1345, per McCombe LJ at [26(4)]; *R (Bridges) v Chief Constable of South Wales Police* [2020] 1 WLR 5064, [2020] EWCA Civ 1058, per Sir Terence Etherton MR, Dame Victoria Sharp PQBD & Singh

the allocations context[301]. Perhaps the most useful statement of the law is in *Hurley & Moore*, where Elias LJ said: 'In short, the decision maker must be clear precisely what the equality implications are when he puts them in the balance, and he must recognise the desirability of achieving them'[302]

It is thus an essential feature of compliance with the PSED that local authorities should identify and consider the consequences of their schemes, particularly where there are discriminatory (or at least potentially discriminatory) effects[303]. As the High Court has put it: 'Any proper examination of the compliance by a public body with the PSED duty must demonstrate how the potentially discriminatory effects of policy decisions have been considered by effective decision makers at a public body'[304].

The High Court has also made the important point that indirect discrimination is, by its nature, often an unintended consequence of allocations rules, and that it can be difficult to spot for that reason[305]. Therefore this process of identifying the impact of a scheme upon protected groups is not necessarily a straightforward exercise. In order to carry this out successfully, local authorities will need to be open-minded about the possibility of adverse effects, rather than adopting a defensive attitude in their assessments. Indeed, it has been held to be a breach of

---

LJ at [175(6)]; *R (Rowley) v Minister for the Cabinet Office* [2022] 1 WLR 1189, [2021] EWHC 2108 (Admin), at [43].

301 See, e.g. *R (Nur) v Birmingham CC (no.1)* [2021] HLR 23, [2021] EWHC 3526 (Admin.) per David Lock QC at [46, 49]; *R (Nur) v Birmingham CC (no.2)* [2021] HLR 41, [2020] EWHC 1138 (Admin), per David Lock QC at [49].

302 [2012] HRLR 13, [2012] EWHC 201 (Admin) at [78].

303 *R (Nur) v Birmingham CC (no.2)* [2021] HLR 41, [2020] EWHC 1138 (Admin), per David Lock QC at [132].

304 *R (Nur) v Birmingham CC (no.1)* [2021] HLR 23, [2021] EWHC 3526 (Admin.) per David Lock QC at [46]. See also [49]..

305 Ibid. at [123].

the PSED that the local authority was merely looking at the functioning of its scheme, rather than considering its possible discriminatory effects[306].

This, of course, involves being frank about the potentially adverse effects. In the first instance decision in *R (H) v Hillingdon*, for example, the High Court held that it was a breach of the PSED for Hillingdon to (wrongly) claim that gender was not relevant to access to social housing[307].

<u>'Due' regard & weight</u>

The PSED requires 'due' regard. The courts have interpreted this as meaning the degree of regard that is 'appropriate in all the circumstances'[308]. In a homelessness case the Supreme Court has expressed its regret that 'this was not a particularly helpful guide', but nevertheless endorsed the point, which (they said) was unavoidable because of Parliament's inclusion of the word 'due' in the statute. Lord Neuberger concluded: 'I do not think it is possible to be more precise or prescriptive, given that the weight and extent of the duty are highly fact-sensitive and dependent on individual judgment'[309].

What this means in practice is that the attention that reviewing officers must pay to the PSED will be different in virtually every case, depending on both the type of case and the overall relevance of the PSED to the issue in dispute. Lord Neuberger is, of course, right to say that what is

---

[306] *R (H) v Ealing LBC* [2016] PTSR 1546, [2016] EWHC 481 (Admin), per HHJ Waksman QC at [108], partially upheld on appeal, with the Court of Appeal holding that Ealing had not looked at the potential adverse effects of its scheme ([2018] PTSR 541, [2017] EWCA Civ 1127, at [115]).

[307] Ibid., per HHK Waksman QC at [109].

[308] *Pieretti v Enfield LBC* [2011] PTSR 565, [2010] EWCA Civ 1104, per Wilson LJ at [33]. For an application in the possession context, see *Luton CHT v Durdana* [2020] HLR 19, [2020] EWCA Civ 445, per Patten LJ at [17-18].

[309] *Hotak v Southwark LBC* [2016] AC 811, [2015] UKSC 30, per Lord Neuberger at [74].

'due' is highly fact-sensitive, and it can be difficult to predict the approach that the courts may take in any given case.

This is clear from the appeal cases in which different judges have dramatically reversed outcomes even when looking at the same facts. In a high-profile challenge to the introduction to automated facial recognition software in South Wales, a Divisional Court (Haddon-Cave LJ and Swift J) said that there was an 'air of unreality' about the PSED ground and dismissed the claim. A notable constitution of the Court of Appeal (Sir Terence Etherton MR, Dame Victoria Sharp PQBD and Singh LJ) reversed them, saying: 'On the contrary, it seems to raise a serious issue of public concern'[310]. In the allocations field, a similar thing happened in *Ward & Gullu*: at first instance the High Court dismissed Ms Ward's challenge but allowed Mr Gullu's (they had brought very similar challenges against the same scheme, although Ms Ward had not specifically raised the PSED), and the Court of Appeal determined that there had been a breach of the PSED in both cases[311].

Importantly, though, in a challenge concerning the old Sex Discrimination Act duty, the High Court appears to have accepted the proposition that: 'In a case where large numbers of vulnerable people, very many of whom fall within one or more of the protected groups, the due regard necessary is very high'[312]. This is a useful point where allocations schemes are concerned, as allocations rules will tend to have an impact on large numbers of groups with protected characteristics.

It is clear is that it is for the local authority and <u>not</u> for the court to decide how much weight to give to the statutory criteria. There is no requirement for the PSED to be given any particular amount of

---

310 *R (Bridges) v Chief Constable of South Wales Police* [2020] 1 WLR 5064, [2020] EWCA Civ 1058 at [173].

311 Court of Appeal case reported at [2019] PTSR 1738, [2019] EWCA Civ 692.

312 *R (Hajrula) v London Councils* [2011] ACD 53, [2011] EWHC 448 (Admin.) per Calvert-Smith J at [62].

weight[313]. As long as there has been 'proper and conscientious focus', the court cannot interfere with the decision 'simply because it would have given greater weight to the equality implications of the decision than did the decision maker'[314]. The battleground, therefore, is usually going to be whether the local authority's PSED exercise was so bad that it actually amounted to a failure to comply with the duty, rather than whether the council merely should have paid more attention to one aspect or another. This is a narrow distinction, but it can be an important one.

Inquiries

Like other public law duties, the PSED implies a duty of 'reasonable' inquiry[315], which requires the local authority to be properly informed before taking a decision[316]. As part of the duty of inquiries the PSED might require public authorities to monitor and release data concerning the impact of their decisions[317], and claimants' representatives may wish

---

[313] *Hackney LBC v Haque* [2017] PTSR 769, [2017] EWCA Civ 4, per Briggs LJ at [23], applied in *R (H) v Ealing LBC (EHRC intervening)* [2018] PTSR 541, [2017] EWCA Civ 1127, per Sir Terence Etherton MR at [111].

[314] *Hotak v Southwark LBC* [2016] AC 811, [2015] UKSC 30, per Lord Neuberger at [75], applied in *R (H) v Ealing LBC (EHRC intervening)* [2018] PTSR 541, [2017] EWCA Civ 1127, per Sir Terence Etherton MR at [112].

[315] *R (Sheakh) v Lambeth LBC* [2022] PTSR 1315, [2022] EWCA Civ 457, per Sir Keith Lindblom SPT, Males & Laing LJJ at [10], citing *Secretary of State for Education & Science v Tameside MBC* [1977] AC 1014. The Court of Appeal in *Sheakh* made the point at [73] that it will only be unlawful for a public authority not to make a particular inquiry if it was irrational for it not to do so.

[316] *R (Brown) v Secretary of State for Work & Pensions* [2009] PTSR 1506, [2008] EWHC 3158 (Admin), per Scott Baker and Aikens LJJ at [85]. In allocations, see *R (Ward & Gullu) v Hillingdon LBC* [2019] PTSR 1738, [2019] EWCA Civ 692, per Lewison LJ at [71].

[317] See, e.g. *R (Unison) v Lord Chancellor* [2016] 1 CMLR 25, [2015] EWCA Civ 935, per Underhill LJ at [121]: the PSED at least requires 'a reasonable and rational view about what effects a particular policy is likely to have'. The failure to collect such impact evidence may be challenged, but (again) only

to put this aspect of the PSED to good use – particularly at the pre-action stages of litigation.

In the allocations field, the High Court has determined that there was a breach of the PSED where the local authority had made no inquiry into how its scheme might impact groups with protected characteristics[318].

Explaining the scheme with candour

In one unfortunate PSED judicial review claim, in which Birmingham City Council failed to engage with the proceedings until a very late stage, the High Court explained that the PSED (in combination with the duty of candour in judicial review) requires local authorities to 'make proper disclosure so that the decision-making process which led up to the adoption of a policy which had these effects can be examined by both the claimant and the court'[319]. In other words, the decision-making process needs to be fairly transparent. It is important to know both whether the local authority was aware of the potential impact of the allocations scheme, and how it factored any such awareness into its decision-making. In the Birmingham case the council failed to demonstrate compliance with the PSED, in that the evidence of a single council employee 'as to why she believes that the Council may have operated this approach' was insufficient[320].

---

on a *Wednesbury* basis: see e.g. *R (Khalsa Academies Trust) v Secretary of State for Education* (unrep.) [2021] EWHC 2660, per Mr Gavin Mansfield QC at [111(ii)].

318 *R (H) v Ealing LBC* [2016] PTSR 1546, [2016] EWHC 481 (Admin), per HHJ Waksman QC at [109, 112], partially upheld on appeal, with the Court of Appeal holding that Ealing had not looked at the potential adverse effects of its scheme ([2018] PTSR 541, [2017] EWCA Civ 1127, at [115]).

319 *R (Nur) v Birmingham CC (no.1)* [2021] HLR 23, [2021] EWHC 3526 (Admin.) per David Lock QC at [49].

320 Ibid.

Anticipating need for services

Consistent with the original intention of the PSED as a proactive duty to avoid discrimination, the High Court has said that the duty (in combination with the Homelessness Act 2002 and section 11 of the Children Act 2004) obliges local authorities to anticipate the levels of service provision that groups with protected characteristics might need, and also to consider what they would need to do to meet those needs[321].

This is a useful principle in housing law, particularly in combination with the Supreme Court's decision in *R (Coll) v Secretary of State for Justice*[322]. *Coll* concerned the inadequate levels of provision of 'approved accommodation' for women being released from prison (when compared with the level of provision for men), and held that this amounted to direct discrimination given that all women faced a greater risk of suffering a detriment (being dispersed to a location that would be a great distance from their homes and families). Given that one of the most important of the PSED's 'equality aims' is the elimination of discrimination, the possibility that inadequate service provision might amount to direct discrimination could be of great relevance.

Monitoring the impact

Where an allocations scheme has been operating for some time, it will be very difficult for a local authority to demonstrate that it has complied with its PSED if it fails to gather any information as to how the scheme is working and whether it has an adverse impact on protected groups[323].

---

321 *R (Bell) v Lambeth LBC* [2022] HLR 45, [2022] EWHC 2008 (Admin), per Hill J at [70, 116].

322 [2017] 1 WLR 2903, [2017] UKSC 40.

323 *R (Nur) v Birmingham CC (no.2)* [2021] HLR 41, [2020] EWHC 1138 (Admin), per David Lock QC at [28].

There needs to be 'some measure of continuing review of the policy so that the local authority understands how it is working out in practice'[324].

Avoiding confirmation bias

Judges will be alert to the possibility that the PSED assessment 'was produced with an "agenda", or that the writer was reasoning backwards from a chosen policy position being defended before a Court'[325]. In a possession case the Court of Appeal said: 'there is an obvious danger of confirmation bias whenever a decision-maker carries out an assessment in relation to a decision that has already been made, rather than in advance; and this is perhaps particularly so in the case of litigation, when costs have already been incurred and the incentive to C pursue the proceedings to a successful conclusion can be very high'[326].

4.6 Consequences of a breach

Where a breach of the PSED has been established, it does not automatically follow that the High Court will grant any remedy in particular, nor any remedy at all.

It is now well-settled that section 31(2A) of the Senior Courts Act 1981 applies to PSED challenges[327]. That section prohibits the Administrative Court from granting a remedy if it is 'highly likely' that the outcome would have been the same if the contravention had not occurred. In other

324 Ibid. at [13]. See also *R (H) v Ealing LBC (EHRC intervening)* [2018] PTSR 541, [2017] EWCA Civ 1127, per Sir Terence Etherton MR at [115].

325 *R (Rowley) v Minister for the Cabinet Office* [2022] 1 WLR 1189, [2021] EWHC 2108 (Admin), per Fordham J at [43].

326 *TM v Metropolitan HT* [2022] 1 WLR 2161, [2021] EWCA Civ 1890, per Nugee LJ at [39]. See also *R (Ward & Gullu) v Hillingdon LBC* [2019] PTSR 1738, [2019] EWCA Civ 692, per Lewison LJ at [76].

327 *Forward v Aldwyck HG* [2020] 1 WLR 584, [2019] EWCA Civ 1334, per Longmore LJ at [36].

words: if the court thinks that it is highly likely that compliance with the PSED would have made no difference, the court cannot grant a remedy.

If, on the other hand, the court concludes that the 'highly likely' test is not satisfied, it may grant a remedy, but remedy in public law proceedings is always a discretionary matter[328].

When applying the 'highly likely' test, it is important to emphasise that the courts should not substitute their own view as to whether compliance with the PSED would or should have made a difference. Instead, the correct approach is for the judge to determine whether the local authority would have done anything differently if the breach had not occurred[329].

The authorities show that the courts are not always willing to grant a remedy for an established breach of the PSED. In *R (H) v Ealing*, for example, the local authority had agreed to carry out a full review of its rules. Even though the council proposed to keep the impugned parts of the policy in operation while that review was being carried out, the Court of Appeal granted no remedy for the breach of the PSED because the council was – by that point – 'alive to the discrimination issue'[330].

In a more recent decision, which followed an important Court of Appeal case that directly concerned the issue of remedy in housing judicial reviews, the PSED ground was treated as something of a sideshow to the issue of whether a remedy should be granted in respect of other grounds. The successful PSED point merely bolstered the High Court's conclusion that a mandatory order should be made[331]. But the court did adopt another recent High Court decision, in which Chamberlain J had

---

328 See e.g. *R (Elkundi) v Birmingham CC* [2022] QB 604, [2022] EWCA Civ 601, per Lewis LJ at [129].

329 *Luton CHT v Durdana* [2020] HLR 19, [2020] EWCA Civ 445, per Patten LJ at [33].

330 *R (H) v Ealing LBC (EHRC intervening)* [2018] PTSR 541, [2017] EWCA Civ 1127, per Sir Terence Etherton MR at [117].

331 *R (Bell) v Lambeth LBC* [2022] HLR 45, [2022] EWHC 2008 (Admin), per Hill J at [116].

considered the question of remedy: where a public body has acted unlawfully the claimant will usually be entitled to a declaration 'to mark the illegality' in cases where no other remedy (such as a quashing order) is appropriate[332].

[332] Ibid. at [87], applying *R (Good Law Project) v Secretary of State for Health and Social Care* [2021] PTSR 1251, [2021] EWHC 346 (Admin).

MORE BOOKS BY LAW BRIEF PUBLISHING

A selection of our other titles available now:-

'A Practical Guide to Parental Alienation in Private and Public Law Children Cases' by Sam King QC & Frankie Shama
'Contested Heritage – Removing Art from Land and Historic Buildings' by Richard Harwood QC, Catherine Dobson, David Sawtell
'The Limits of Separate Legal Personality: When Those Running a Company Can Be Held Personally Liable for Losses Caused to Third Parties Outside of the Company' by Dr Mike Wilkinson
'A Practical Guide to Transgender Law' by Robin Moira White & Nicola Newbegin
'Artificial Intelligence – The Practical Legal Issues (2nd Edition)' by John Buyers
'A Practical Guide to Residential Freehold Conveyancing' by Lorraine Richardson
'A Practical Guide to Pensions on Divorce for Lawyers' by Bryan Scant
'A Practical Guide to Challenging Sham Marriage Allegations in Immigration Law' by Priya Solanki
'A Practical Guide to Legal Rights in Scotland' by Sarah-Jane Macdonald
'A Practical Guide to New Build Conveyancing' by Paul Sams & Rebecca East
'A Practical Guide to Defending Barristers in Disciplinary Cases' by Marc Beaumont
'A Practical Guide to Inherited Wealth on Divorce' by Hayley Trim
'A Practical Guide to Practice Direction 12J and Domestic Abuse in Private Law Children Proceedings' by Rebecca Cross & Malvika Jaganmohan
'A Practical Guide to Confiscation and Restraint' by Narita Bahra QC, John Carl Townsend, David Winch
'A Practical Guide to the Law of Forests in Scotland' by Philip Buchan
'A Practical Guide to Health and Medical Cases in Immigration Law' by Rebecca Chapman & Miranda Butler
'A Practical Guide to Bad Character Evidence for Criminal Practitioners by Aparna Rao
'A Practical Guide to Extradition Law post-Brexit' by Myles Grandison et al

'A Practical Guide to Hoarding and Mental Health for Housing Lawyers' by Rachel Coyle
'A Practical Guide to Psychiatric Claims in Personal Injury – 2nd Edition' by Liam Ryan
'Stephens on Contractual Indemnities' by Richard Stephens
'A Practical Guide to the EU Succession Regulation' by Richard Frimston
'A Practical Guide to Solicitor and Client Costs – 2nd Edition' by Robin Dunne
'Constructive Dismissal – Practice Pointers and Principles' by Benjimin Burgher
'A Practical Guide to Religion and Belief Discrimination Claims in the Workplace' by Kashif Ali
'A Practical Guide to the Law of Medical Treatment Decisions' by Ben Troke
'Fundamental Dishonesty and QOCS in Personal Injury Proceedings: Law and Practice' by Jake Rowley
'A Practical Guide to the Law in Relation to School Exclusions' by Charlotte Hadfield & Alice de Coverley
'A Practical Guide to Divorce for the Silver Separators' by Karin Walker
'The Right to be Forgotten – The Law and Practical Issues' by Melissa Stock
'A Practical Guide to Planning Law and Rights of Way in National Parks, the Broads and AONBs' by James Maurici QC, James Neill et al
'A Practical Guide to Election Law' by Tom Tabori
'A Practical Guide to the Law in Relation to Surrogacy' by Andrew Powell
'A Practical Guide to Claims Arising from Fatal Accidents – 2nd Edition' by James Patience
'A Practical Guide to the Ownership of Employee Inventions – From Entitlement to Compensation' by James Tumbridge & Ashley Roughton
'A Practical Guide to Asbestos Claims' by Jonathan Owen & Gareth McAloon
'A Practical Guide to Stamp Duty Land Tax in England and Northern Ireland' by Suzanne O'Hara
'A Practical Guide to the Law of Farming Partnerships' by Philip Whitcomb
'Covid-19, Homeworking and the Law – The Essential Guide to Employment and GDPR Issues' by Forbes Solicitors
'Covid-19 and Criminal Law – The Essential Guide' by Ramya Nagesh
'Covid-19 and Family Law in England and Wales – The Essential Guide' by Safda Mahmood

'A Practical Guide to the Law of Unlawful Eviction and Harassment – 2nd Edition' by Stephanie Lovegrove
'Covid-19, Brexit and the Law of Commercial Leases – The Essential Guide' by Mark Shelton
'A Practical Guide to Costs in Personal Injury Claims – 2nd Edition' by Matthew Hoe
'A Practical Guide to the General Data Protection Regulation (GDPR) – 2nd Edition' by Keith Markham
'Ellis on Credit Hire – Sixth Edition' by Aidan Ellis & Tim Kevan
'A Practical Guide to Working with Litigants in Person and McKenzie Friends in Family Cases' by Stuart Barlow
'Protecting Unregistered Brands: A Practical Guide to the Law of Passing Off' by Lorna Brazell
'A Practical Guide to Secondary Liability and Joint Enterprise Post-Jogee' by Joanne Cecil & James Mehigan
'A Practical Guide to the Pre-Action RTA Claims Protocol for Personal Injury Lawyers' by Antonia Ford
'A Practical Guide to Neighbour Disputes and the Law' by Alexander Walsh
'A Practical Guide to Forfeiture of Leases' by Mark Shelton
'A Practical Guide to Coercive Control for Legal Practitioners and Victims' by Rachel Horman
'A Practical Guide to Rights Over Airspace and Subsoil' by Daniel Gatty
'Tackling Disclosure in the Criminal Courts – A Practitioner's Guide' by Narita Bahra QC & Don Ramble
'A Practical Guide to the Law of Driverless Cars – Second Edition' by Alex Glassbrook, Emma Northey & Scarlett Milligan
'A Practical Guide to TOLATA Claims' by Greg Williams
'A Practical Guide to Elderly Law – 2nd Edition' by Justin Patten
'A Practical Guide to Responding to Housing Disrepair and Unfitness Claims' by Iain Wightwick
'A Practical Guide to the Construction and Rectification of Wills and Trust Instruments' by Edward Hewitt
'A Practical Guide to the Law of Bullying and Harassment in the Workplace' by Philip Hyland
'How to Be a Freelance Solicitor: A Practical Guide to the SRA-Regulated Freelance Solicitor Model' by Paul Bennett

'A Practical Guide to Prison Injury Claims' by Malcolm Johnson
'A Practical Guide to the Small Claims Track - 2nd Edition' by Dominic Bright
'A Practical Guide to Advising Clients at the Police Station' by Colin Stephen McKeown-Beaumont
'A Practical Guide to Antisocial Behaviour Injunctions' by Iain Wightwick
'Practical Mediation: A Guide for Mediators, Advocates, Advisers, Lawyers, and Students in Civil, Commercial, Business, Property, Workplace, and Employment Cases' by Jonathan Dingle with John Sephton
'The Mini-Pupillage Workbook' by David Boyle
'A Practical Guide to Crofting Law' by Brian Inkster
'A Practical Guide to Spousal Maintenance' by Liz Cowell
'A Practical Guide to the Law of Domain Names and Cybersquatting' by Andrew Clemson
'A Practical Guide to the Law of Gender Pay Gap Reporting' by Harini Iyengar
'A Practical Guide to the Rights of Grandparents in Children Proceedings' by Stuart Barlow
'NHS Whistleblowing and the Law' by Joseph England
'Employment Law and the Gig Economy' by Nigel Mackay & Annie Powell
'A Practical Guide to Noise Induced Hearing Loss (NIHL) Claims' by Andrew Mckie, Ian Skeate, Gareth McAloon
'An Introduction to Beauty Negligence Claims – A Practical Guide for the Personal Injury Practitioner' by Greg Almond
'Intercompany Agreements for Transfer Pricing Compliance' by Paul Sutton
'Zen and the Art of Mediation' by Martin Plowman
'A Practical Guide to the SRA Principles, Individual and Law Firm Codes of Conduct 2019 – What Every Law Firm Needs to Know' by Paul Bennett
'A Practical Guide to Adoption for Family Lawyers' by Graham Pegg
'A Practical Guide to Industrial Disease Claims' by Andrew Mckie & Ian Skeate
'A Practical Guide to Redundancy' by Philip Hyland
'A Practical Guide to Vicarious Liability' by Mariel Irvine
'A Practical Guide to Applications for Landlord's Consent and Variation of Leases' by Mark Shelton
'A Practical Guide to Relief from Sanctions Post-Mitchell and Denton' by Peter Causton

'A Practical Guide to Equity Release for Advisors' by Paul Sams
'A Practical Guide to Financial Services Claims' by Chris Hegarty
'The Law of Houses in Multiple Occupation: A Practical Guide to HMO Proceedings' by Julian Hunt
'Occupiers, Highways and Defective Premises Claims: A Practical Guide Post-Jackson – 2nd Edition' by Andrew Mckie
'A Practical Guide to Financial Ombudsman Service Claims' by Adam Temple & Robert Scrivenor
'A Practical Guide to Advising Schools on Employment Law' by Jonathan Holden
'A Practical Guide to Running Housing Disrepair and Cavity Wall Claims: 2nd Edition' by Andrew Mckie & Ian Skeate
'A Practical Guide to Holiday Sickness Claims – 2nd Edition' by Andrew Mckie & Ian Skeate
'Arguments and Tactics for Personal Injury and Clinical Negligence Claims' by Dorian Williams
'A Practical Guide to Drone Law' by Rufus Ballaster, Andrew Firman, Eleanor Clot
'A Practical Guide to Compliance for Personal Injury Firms Working With Claims Management Companies' by Paul Bennett
'RTA Allegations of Fraud in a Post-Jackson Era: The Handbook – 2nd Edition' by Andrew Mckie
'RTA Personal Injury Claims: A Practical Guide Post-Jackson' by Andrew Mckie
'On Experts: CPR35 for Lawyers and Experts' by David Boyle
'An Introduction to Personal Injury Law' by David Boyle

www.ingramcontent.com/pod-product-compliance
Lightning Source LLC
LaVergne TN
LVHW022102200926
848481LV00003B/1029
9781914608605